HEAD START

Teach Your Toddler to Learn

KEN ADAMS

WITHDRAWN

MICHAEL O'MARA BOOKS LIMITED

First published in Great Britain in 1992
by Michael O'Mara Books Limited,
9 Lion Yard, Tremadoc Road, London SW4 7NQ

A CIP catalogue record for this book is available from the
British Library.

ISBN 1-85479-171-0

Edited by Georgina Evans
Designed by Mick Keates

Typeset by Florencetype Ltd, Kewstoke, Avon
Printed and bound in England by Clays Ltd, St Ives plc

ACKNOWLEDGEMENTS

I would like to thank Mrs. B. Lister for her help in
producing written music for the tunes on pages 62
and 64; and Schools Council Project for allowing us
to reproduce the drawings on pages 135–139 from
Talking and Learning by Joan Tough (Ward Lock
Educational in association with Drake Educational
Associates, 1977); and to cartoonist Maddocks and
his book Cartooning for Beginners (Michael
O'Mara Books, 1992) for help with the
illustrations.

CONTENTS

CHAPTER ONE

INTRODUCTION

'Give me the child until he is seven and I will give you the man.' Piaget

'It's exactly 2.56 p.m.', lisped the two-year-old.

The family-clinic doctor swayed on her stool for a few seconds, totally bemused. 'I don't believe it', she finally stuttered. 'He reads from my medical book, counts like a computer and tells the time to the minute. In 30 years of practice . . .' Her voice trailed off, as her mind flew back over the years, remembering countless toddlers and their behaviour.

'Please get me some help for him', I pleaded.

She nodded and smiled a reassuring smile. But there was no help for my little son from the powers that be. I was desolate. Where were all the experts when I needed them? Didn't they care?

Twelve years on, I knew the truth: there are no experts on pre-school children available to advise parents. In fact, nobody is clear what to do with a precocious toddler. An educational psychologist once said to me, 'He's bored. So what? Everybody gets bored, don't they?' My son was so active mentally that he was still on the go at midnight and up at 6.30 the next morning. I tried the local playgroup but they had only vague ideas about play, a few toys and custard creams for the children's mid-morning break. Ten miles away, I heard, was an excellent private nursery school with good facilities, where they taught pre-school children to count, to read and aimed to fulfil their potential intellectually, as well as socially. I had little money and could not afford to pay. The only alternative was to use my experience as a teacher and develop a programme of home learning to satisfy my son's eager mind. Eighteen months later he was academically at the end of primary school. Yet he had spent less than half-an-hour a day 'playing' at school-related activities. It was something every mother could easily cope with in the normal course of bringing up her child.

My son eventually passed GCE 'O' Levels at eight and 'A' levels at nine, and his two younger brothers have since gained scholarships to public schools. I have watched many toddlers with apparently average intelligence develop into bright, successful and confident school children with the help of the advice that is now contained in these pages *and* with the encouragement of their mothers. What is truly remarkable is that this success is not just the result of increased knowledge. Children who at one time thought slower than many others now match them for speed of reasoning. Mental stimulation breeds a mind that is more alert, quicker thinking and with a ready ability to concentrate.

My book, *Your Child Can Be Top Of The Class*, proved that it was possible for children aged five and over to do significantly better at school than most teachers and parents believed possible if my learning methods were followed. This new book is designed to have the same effect on pre-school children. At the moment when a child has the ability to absorb more information rapidly than at any other time in his or her life, a child can be irretrievably handicapped by bad teaching or having none at all.

In *Head Start* I put forward a foolproof way of giving your child a head start. A potentially brilliant child can be given a kick start that will take him or her high up the academic ladder. This book can make all the difference to the child with ordinary ability in preparing for school. Instead of wasting the first year or two of schooling (which can never be made up) the child can demonstrate an amazing ability to learn from the start by learning *how* to learn. The confidence thus gained provides great encouragement and enables a child with average learning ability to be counted among the brightest.

Developing Intelligence

One-to-one teaching by a parent at home is indeed extremely effective in developing mind skills and inculcating knowlege into memory that will result in later academic success. However, a parent needs to determine what her or his child knows and to know how to build on that experience in memory. A parent needs to know not only what environment to provide to further intellectual development, but also to know why certain activities fulfil this. It is not enough to say that play is important, so let your child play. What does a pre-school child play with? Does he play on his push-bike outside or with teddy bears inside?

These seem to be questions about limiting a child's freedom but is a child truly free who is at a disadvantage in coping with important aspects of the real world, particularly schooling? He may be restricted by his inability to master abstract work in the confines of the classrom. No amount of free play can provide him with the knowledge to overcome this.

Within these pages, therefore, are set down the whys and wherefores of learning and of teaching a pre-school child. By assessing your child's stage of intellectual development and building on it *before* school you will give him a clear head start, a start from which he will never look back.

CHAPTER TWO

HOW DOES A TODDLER LEARN?

'Hello, Mummy', said the ten-week-old baby. The room full of adults stood silent for a few seconds and then exploded with what amounted to a standing ovation for baby Tiffany. In the next half-an-hour she took several curtain calls.

This was not a spontaneous outburst by the tiny baby. Three to four weeks earlier she had surprised us all by saying, 'Hello', very clearly in a perfect imitation of her auntie's high-pitched voice. Before this, at least a hundred times, mother and mother's friends had sat with her and mouthed the words. She

watched, this little bundle of quick-eyed wonderment, moving her lips, poking out her tongue in imitation, and making near-correct sounds, until that day when everything came together.

So how do small children learn? They certainly learn by imitation. Three-year-olds in particular are notorious for trotting out oft-repeated phrases of their elders, sometimes to their parents' great distress. Repetition is important, and also the presentation of a clearly defined item or its representation. But this item must always be presented in the same form. Early readers see ɑ and a as completely different letters and where adults can discern variations in the patterns presented to them, children cannot, simply because they have not been taught those variations. Even variations in the ways that letters are written are not always recognised:

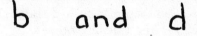

With wider experience, and consequent practice, these variations become incorporated into memory and associated with each other. But initially we should appreciate that our view of the world is *not* that of the child's. They often associate sounds with similar looking letters:

b and d

They confuse directions:

⊣ is 4

And they attach a far narrower range of meanings to words. 'More' often means 'taller than' or 'longer than' to a young child, not greater quantity.

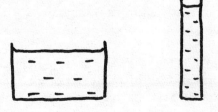

Practising Sounds

There is a prerequisite to a baby saying, 'Hello, Mummy.' For several weeks Tiffany Jo had been making sounds on her own, or trying to copy other sounds her mother made. 'Ah-goo' occurred regularly. When the baby's memory had assimilated the representations of a certain number of sounds and mouth movements, she was able to link the new mouth movement and sound into the established body of knowledge or *schemata* in memory. This had meaning, although of a superficial kind. She had no idea that 'Hello, Mummy' was a greeting, or even what a Mummy was. The words had meaning only in that she recognised the mouth shape, tongue position, and the sound associated with them.

A body of knowledge is the representation of a set of experiences in memory that will give meaning to a similar environmental influence. In a young child, Mother's voice would link with memory through a body of knowledge that included recognition of sound, the various modulations of voice and a recognition of 'mother' and all that implies. As I have said above, bodies of knowledge are also called 'schemata' or, more simply, groups of related concepts, and such a system in memory has implications in learning. Knowledge should be placed in related groups for learning and some concepts cannot be properly learnt unless certain information is in memory.

So it can be seen that these established bodies of knowledge in memory are crucial to the learning process. What schemata or concrete groups of related concepts are present in memory will determine what level of meaning we will be able to give to incoming information. Attempts to create meanings of a deeper kind, essentially those related to real-life experience, and to effect links between a variety of groups of concepts, both superficial and deep, will ultimately result in greater creativity and an increased ability to 'think' well. In turn, the very capability to think well gives confidence to the thinker stimulating interest in her own adventurous thought.

Potential

Two minds starting life with the same potential can end life with vastly different sets of related concepts and linkages. It may be that one will have extensive networks dealing with skills and colloquialisms and become a person who is successful in certain social circles and areas of work. The other may not have the verbal ability of the first, or have his or her 'intelligence' in skilled labour, but he or she may have developed thinking abilities that have resulted in a successful academic career.

Concrete Images

'What colour is snow?' I asked Nikita, aged three, one frosty morning. She did not reply. I asked the question again.

'It's red,' she said.

I bent down and plucked some frost from the blades of grass at our feet. 'Look,' I said, 'This is like snow. It's white. Have you never seen snow before?'

'Yes,' she said, 'but I forgot.'

She knew her colours, she knew the meaning of the question but she had seen snow on one day only, sometime before. The knowledge was not firmly established in memory. Now, in the middle of that twinkling sea of white, touching the icy frost and talking about snow, would make the experience memorable. There would be easy links with real-life experiences in memory, experiences of texture, cold and colour that were easily recalled to give additional meaning. Later, I asked her again what colour snow was and she replied, wickedly, 'It's purple,' but there was a half-grin on her face.

'You know, really, don't you?' I said, and she giggled at the trick she was playing on me.

Meanings

A very young child initially needs to give meaning to her experience so that she can use it to her best advantage. The experience may be a mother's smile, the teat in a baby's mouth, or the sound of a rattle. A vast network of related concepts is built up representing the input of experience and giving meaning to that experience whenever it is encountered again. Gradually, the young infant learns to interpret the language with which close adults are attempting to communicate. She learns through all the senses the meanings of words and phrases, and also the inferences behind those words, phrases and associated gestures. Later, at about three years of age, the way in which a parent explains the meanings of words will have a lasting effect, because it is through the deeper meanings that much new experience can link to and build upon. In particular, concepts build on concepts, and the absence of a prerequisite structure or basis can hinder the development of thoughtful intelligence.

It is not only the learning of concrete words which is important at this stage but also the learning of words with *abstract* meanings. Children at school struggle more with abstract meaning than they do with concrete meaning. 'Mercy' is a considerably more difficult concept to grasp than 'dog'. 'Mercy' links with other complex and difficult concepts such as 'forgiveness'. These are not easily visualised because to give deep meaning to a word like 'mercy' it has to be related to an experience in memory. A dog is a living, breathing, three-dimensional object and from such the mind will have no difficulty in creating an appropriate mental image to link with the bodies of knowledge in memory.

Abstract Words

How then can abstract words and phrases be learnt, since the best learning experience for a toddler is real-life experience? Nobody would advocate deliberately giving small children experience of hate, jealousy, misery and so on. However, since such words represent human emotions, to which much other experience can be linked, clear mental images do need to be created. One way a parent can communicate meaning to their child is to point to incidents in a toddler's life, or refer to displays of emotion in fairy tales and nursery rhymes. Films and cartoons also create powerful and memorable images and it is through stories in general that experience in the form of related concepts can be linked into memory. The child who reads widely feeds on the life-blood of human experience.

Drawing Together Experiences

There also needs to be a drawing together of experiences, sometimes very wide-ranging, so that possible pathways to undiscovered experience may be realised. This is the essence of creativity and can be achieved in many ways through various forms of play, discussion with mother, art, model-making, music and drama. Attempts to solve problematical situations and investigations will encourage this process in a child, but it is a child's own innate drive to creative thought that will result in the most satisfying and productive discoveries.

Established Knowledge

By three years of age there are certain bodies of knowledge established in memory. They are, in the main, associated with real life. Your child knows how to walk, how to hold a spoon and eat; she also knows that if she climbs too high she could fall and hurt herself. It is unlikely, however, that she is able to share ten sweets fairly between herself and her brother and she will not know if it is tea-time on Thursday or not.

Words that a pre-school child knows are invariably spoken. She knows few written ones and there is little knowledge of abstract word meanings. A lot of talk is colloquial, copied from adults and older children, as is much behaviour. The imitative element is predominant. This means that attempts by parents to preserve so-called freedom of expression in speech and behaviour, and development of the 'natural man' within their child, are of little avail. The environment is itself an imposition that determines what bodies of knowledge are created in memory. Freedom of expression and the so-called 'natural' within a child can often only be fully expressed after instruction by a parent-tutor has supplied the knowledge necessary for survival in the modern world.

The Learning Process

In understanding how children learn it is useful to think of the mind as an information processing unit. Information enters through the sense organs, is coded and passed to the brain where it can be stored for a short time (in temporary or short-term memory). A search is then instigated in long-term memory for 'matching' items, and when a match has been made the input information has meaning. What type of knowledge is present in long-term memory will determine the depth of meaning that can be ascribed to new information. A body of knowledge is the representation of a set of experiences in memory that will give meaning to some environmental influence.

'Daddy has gone to work,' said Mary's mother one morning. Later, Mary had Daddy's work place pointed out to her. 'That's where Daddy works,' she was told. Now Mary knows that the big white building in the centre of town is where Daddy goes when he is not at home.

The new information about 'Daddy's work' has been linked to a 'house' in the town centre, and also to the knowledge of Daddy's absence. Whenever Daddy is not home and somebody asks, 'Where is Daddy?' she says, 'At work,' even if it is midday on Sunday, or 11.30 at night. She does not even think in terms of work as a concept, and until she does, cannot build on this deeper aspect of meaning. This is why, when talking to your child, it is important to explain generalised concepts like work, tree and home, because many items of knowledge can later be linked to them.

A Model of Learning

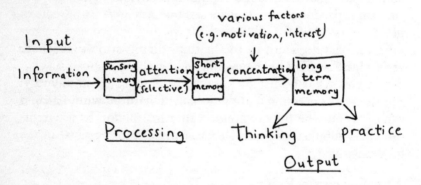

Learning will focus on four main areas:

(1) **Input** Presentation and the selection of information.

(2) **Processing** The internal operations leading to creation of meaning.

(3) **Output** External practice to cement new information in long-term memory. Coupled with thinking and the attempt to draw together separated items of knowledge by establishing links.

Input can include incidental learning or unguided learning (although the very placing of a child in a particular environment will 'guide' her learning), and directed learning, usually involving selected experiences that a parent decides are useful for their child. Social training is directed learning: 'Don't touch the cooker, it's hot.' 'Play nicely with your friend.'

Academic Advantage

Many parents now see the benefit of consciously providing experience, especially academic-related experience, that will give academic advantage to the rapidly developing child of three to six years old. Developing this aspect of meanings, as distinct from real-world concrete meanings, makes it easier for a teacher to link schoolwork to abstract related concepts in a child's memory. Furthermore, a child who has such experience is perceived as more intelligent than the others. The teacher's perception transmits itself to the child and increases her confidence, stimulating interest and thus aiding concentration. Concentration itself drives knowledge into long-term memory by intensifying the search for matching items.

The Creation of Meanings

The struggle for survival in the world leads a young child to create a body of knowledge in its mind that will give meaning to the experiences it encounters in its environment. The child tries to make sense of her world by linking input to something in memory. Past experience will determine how fully she can appreciate the situation and how well she reacts to it.

The first phase in this process is the creation of a mental image. But what is a mental image? If somebody says 'shoe' to me I produce a succession of images in my mind. I see a picture of a 'shoe', of different types of 'shoe' but I can also appreciate what a shoe feels like to put on my foot, a sense of the three-dimensional form of it, and the protection it gives to the foot. There are links to foot, sock, toes, shoe-shops, the cost of shoes and a whole body of knowledge that I have built up in association with the one word 'shoe'. All these 'senses' of form and touch can be considered to be mental images: sometimes there is an immediate associated visual form, and sometimes there is not. Initially, when we hear the word 'shoe' we have an instant sense of its meaning without being able to attach clear pictures to it, or to describe with words. This 'sense' of something is the mental image, the creation of meaning without a clear picture or formation of description. These mental pictures take longer to create but seem to be the mind's way of cementing links to long-term memory through practice. 'Skimming' for meaning is the knee-jerk way of creating an instant response to the environment.

Pictures and Mental Images

'Skimming' for meaning does, in fact, seem to be the way we operate in everyday life. Even a three-year-old does this but has fewer related concepts in memory. However, to learn well the creation of clear pictures is essential and some children have a greater ability to create such pictures than others. The highly indistinct mental image in 'skimming' for meaning is insufficient for developing deep meaning. It is recognising the form but not the substance. This is why time and concentration need to be applied for good quality learning to take place.

Developing Patterns of Thought

Martin, aged three, picked up a large stone the other day. 'What's that?' I asked.

'It's a rock,' he said.

'What is it like?' I continued.

'It's dirty,' he said, brushing off some earth.

I persisted, 'Where did it come from?'

'The dustman brought it,' he said, very positively. (He knew this because he had just seen the dustman in the back garden, emptying the bin.)

A child of three attributes meaning to a stone on the basis of how heavy it feels on his hand, its size, texture, shape and colour (even if he cannot *name* the colour). These rather superficial bodies of knowledge might be linked with other related concepts like the one that prompts the question: 'Will this hurt if I drop it on my foot?' or 'How will this fit into some game I want to play?' He may even use it to try to 'pin' some unfortunate earthworm. However, patterns of thought of a more valuable kind and those that will be of use academically, need to be consciously developed by a parent. Eventually, such thinking is self-perpetuating because the establishing of these sort of related concepts in memory and their continual usage will make it the director of how future thinking should take place.

Limitations

There are certain limitations on what pre-school children can learn. They are limited physically. Jonathan can draw most of his letters at three years of age, whereas Tony, at nearly five, has been struggling for months to write 12 of the letters. Some children have an innate ability to do certain things. Jonathan's parents are highly gifted and qualified artists and their son's ability to copy line and form developed at an early age. He also learns quickly anyway, having that mysterious ability to extract core learning elements and create clear pictures in his mind.

Even when so-called slower children have material presented clearly to them, they are still distracted relatively easily either by some irrelevance in that material or by something in the near surroundings.

Some young children also have fewer bodies of knowledge in their memory than others, particularly when parents have not read to them, talked to them and provided a stimulating environment for learning. There are other limitations which are effectively dictated by social class. Within certain social groupings whole patterns of thought can be inculcated into a child which represent fairly superficial meanings. She is highly intelligent within that group but is not adapted for survival within other social groups. Children who learn the language and behaviour of the streets and are street-wise, playing outside for much of their young lives, have great difficulty adjusting to the cloistered, middle-class dominated environment at school. They simply do not have the relevant related concepts in their memories to link to new, more abstract information and so create deep meanings. It is not enough to know 'how' or to have developed practical skills. There is great power in knowing 'that' or about things in general, particularly in school life.

Play and Your Pre-School Child

Young children spend most of their time playing. So, what is the value of play? Certainly, it is important to develop a playful approach to learning because this will stimulate interest and aid concentration. Bodies of knowledge will be developed in memory which associate pleasure with learning, just as strong links between punishment and learning will develop distaste.

Furthermore in play the limits of actions can be tested and tried out with relative impunity. Play reflects a child's need to practise what has been observed and to relate this new knowledge to that already established in memory. Through play there is the opportunity to try out behaviour that in real life could never be 'played'.

'Playing' with language is of crucial importance to development. Unless this occurs on a regular basis, word meanings and meanings of inference and gesture may be lost. Whether imitating real life, or imaginative, play is a stimulus for language growth; experience communicated through language is essential for success in school.

SUMMARY

Your pre-school child will profit academically from the establishment of bodies of knowledge or related concepts in memory that reflect both concrete and abstract word meanings, together with a comprehension of inference in speech, gesture and writing, and also of investigation, number and problem solving. The wider the range of such experience and the deeper the meanings developed, the brighter the child will be perceived to be.

It is not enough for a child to develop sets of skills to succeed in modern society, academic success is often a passport to a professional career. One can become a medical doctor or solicitor only through the academic system and the knowledge for such work includes not only skills but the ability to reason, assess and inform. In life we can survive with skills alone but begin to live in a meaningful way only through the acquiring of deeper knowledge. There is a very real danger that your child will learn to live at a superficial level, creating only images in her mind that represent skills, in a figurative sense knowing how to turn the door handle but having no mental picture of the workings of the lock.

CHAPTER THREE

HOW SHOULD A PARENT TEACH A PRE-SCHOOL CHILD?

There are two basic questions that parents have directed to me over the years. The first is, 'What is the best way to teach my child?', and the second is, 'What should such a young child be taught?' The first question is, in the main, a psychological one while the second is philosophical and, in spite of lack of *concrete* evidence, most parents require a *concrete* answer.

In an attempt to answer the psychological question, many years ago I embarked on a programme of one-to-one teaching. The pupils were of a wide age range and ability. I did not confine myself to any one category because I felt that the learning process was similar across the board. Older and more educated pupils were physically more sophisticated and had therefore more manipulative skills, and, of course, they had more knowledge than younger children. However, the difference in intellectual ability was, in the main, due to a greater understanding of concepts in the maturer pupils. I considered it impossible to investigate learning by modelling such an investigation along the lines of the physical sciences as there are too many variables in the learning process. Observation and thought were powerful weapons and the quality of thought, that is being able to think deeply, was crucial. The best subject for study was, of course, oneself, especially to corroborate what seemed to be occurring in others.

Deciding what a toddler should be taught involves value judgements. Most parents consider that a small proportion of the day should be set aside for 'bookish' pursuits, especially after a story has been read to them – counting the steps to bedtime, or having the meanings of various items explained – but there is no clear rationale behind this thinking. Many parents have heard that play is valuable and they provide toys, including educational toys, that seem to contribute towards a contented child.

The philosophic issues are far from clear-cut and many vexed and contentious issues are raised when one asks what should be taught, if anything, to a pre-school child? It has never seemed to me a possibility that a child below the age of five is not ready for certain learning activities simply because he is too young.

So, the questions tumble out: should home learning involve mostly creative play? How much 'abstract' thought development should there be? Is it necessary to teach traditional academic skills to this age group? Along with many parents I feel it is reasonable to see the whole of life as an educative process. Since the pre-school years provide the foundation of knowledge to which all other knowledge is linked, some thought should be given to preparing a child for school life. It is up to a parent to decide how much time and effort he or she is prepared to give to developing the pre-school child's intellect. When that has been decided, a parent must spread the umbrella wide when deciding how a child should spend his time. This not only ensures that latent talent is unearthed but also that a wide variety of related concepts are developed in memory so that school experience can be easily assimilated. Concentrating on Reading, Writing and Arithmetic does not ensure this but neither does a slavish adherence to free play principles. The aim of education should be the encouragement of good thinking practice through problem solving, investigation and creative exercise.

Patterns of Learning

A pre-school child is learning *how* to learn. Good habits fostered at an early age are, themselves, stored for reference in memory. When you place a finger on a word it focuses your child's attention on that word, sending its coded representation, that is the form in which experience is transmitted through the nervous system, into short-term memory. When you ask the question, 'What does this word say?', it should cause your child to develop a level of concentration that will match the word image to something corresponding in memory. This will create only superficial meaning, since it will involve sight and sound alone. When you ask, 'What does this word mean?' greater concentration is required to search for a match at a conceptual level and create deeper meaning.

A work like 'danger' will illustrate how these internal processes operate. All image formation is a reflection of real-life experience but it is the conscious formation of a clear mental picture that enables this learning. Holding such a picture strengthens the link with real-life experience in long-term memory. It is, in effect, a form of practice, which, if repeated enough, will result in *overlearning*. This is the practising of a skill or memorisation of an item well beyond the point where it seems to have been incorporated into long-term memory. It generally ensures instant recall when required.

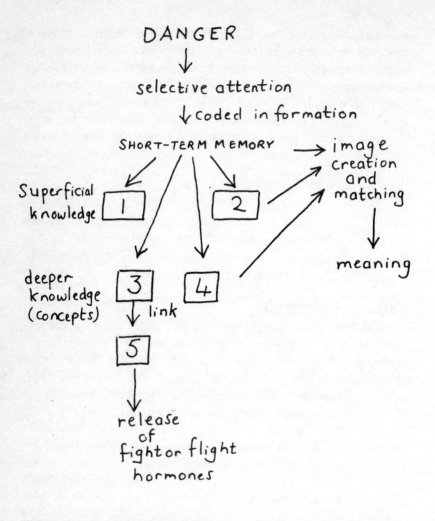

1) Word and letter *form*.

2) Word and letter *sounds*.

3) DANGER means drowning, burning, electrocuting, etc.

4) Recognition of dangerous environments/situations – ponds, busy road, etc.

5) Hormones released in the body

Your child can be taught to ask himself questions and these ease concentration. This is especially true of 'What does this mean?' questions. Once a search at the deeper levels of long-term memory has been initiated, half the learning battle has been won. Quicker children seem to have an instinctive ability to delve into the mass of deeper-level groups of related concepts through effective mental picture formation. They also have greater conceptual awareness.

Real-Life Meaning

Most three-year-olds have a considerable range of related concepts from real life in long-term memory and also a certain number concerned with spoken speech. From child to child there will, of course, be a difference in the variety of experience. Children who have played outdoors for most of their walking life and had little communication with their parents, will have markedly different sets of related concepts to those who have played indoors more often and have been talked and read to by an adult. Without the help and encouragement of an adult a child's language may remain at a level which is only a little removed from rudimentary signalling. Some children, from birth, will have had the potential to be physically more adept, to be better talkers, or to learn faster in general. They seem to be born with greater perceptual abilities, being able to create deep mental pictures in their minds and attribute meaning to experience.

Once you have the information as to what your child knows you will have an idea of what further experience will easily add to memory stock. Thus, the first rule for teaching your child is know your child. The information in chapters 4, 5 and 6 will aid you in this, but, basically, you are the one who knows your child best.

Listing Your Child's Capabilities

List what your child can do under the following categories:

a) **Drawing lines** The ability to recognise patterns will give a good guide to your child's ability to write and begin to read.

$$| \quad | = \quad \backslash \quad \backslash \quad / \quad /$$

b) **Copying sounds** Has your child the ability to copy sounds that you make? Try letter sounds for accuracy. Some children, for example those from the Asian community, have difficulty. For example, *w* in Urdu is pronounced like a *v*.

c) **The ability to repeat words** Say simple words to your child. Check that he can say words like 'man' correctly. This is simply a test for errors in speech reproduction.

d) **Word meanings** Use the words in the relevant chapter to test for word meaning. (This is a *verbal* test, not a reading one.) Words representing certain concrete objects, e.g. chair, table, bus, car, should be known by about three years of age. Language is a very effective tool to communicate meaning.

e) **Copying actions** See if your child can copy actions – raise your arm and see if he can do likewise. The knowledge of left and right is very rarely known by three- or four-year-olds, and to raise the identical left or right arm as a parent is very difficult.

f) **Assessing physical development** See the relevant chapters.

g) **Singing in tune/sense of rhythm** This will give a good guide to musical ability. Very short songs are the most valuable.

h) **Understanding inference in speech** What does the giant man mean when he says, 'I'll grind your bones to make my bread'? Comprehension of stories, of soap operas on television and of every-day relationships greatly extend a child's knowledge of the world. He needs to know that James is simply jealous when he says, 'I don't like you' because he has a toy that James wants himself. You will need to gauge his appreciation of human nature and understanding of colloquial speech.

i) **Dramatic ability** Get your child to act out passages from fairy tales. Some very small children have great natural talent that can be used to develop intelligence by experiencing a range of feelings through acting them out.

j) **Counting ability** Most three-year-olds have been taught to count 1, 2, 3, or even up to 5 or more. It is extremely important that he learns that you count only one of a kind.

$$3 \text{ cows} + 2 \text{ sheep} = 5 \text{ cows-sheep?}$$

k) **Play** No parent should underestimate the value of play. Has your child yet learnt to play with models of real-life objects – roadways, garages, houses — and toys such as dolls, marbles and so on? If he or she has not, then much experience may be lost because play is practice, it is testing limits, and it develops imagination. These new meanings and links within long-term memory are extremely important.

A three-year-old should also be beginning to play alongside others of his own age. A child who is able to relate well to other children and adults will find his path through life is easier, as long as he remains true to himself. As one mother said to me, 'I don't mind if he ain't bright but does he have manners?' He was, in fact, extremely polite and caring. The same could not be said for the famous five-year-old son of an American lady psychotherapist, who appeared on television with me once. He had an IQ of 200 but his mother did not appear to believe in correction or guidance and the result seemed to be an extremely unruly, ill-tempered and unsociable child. He had to be dragged, screaming, from a live television programme.

Is your child creative in play? Small children make up their own stories, often including real-life speech and items they have seen on television or in films, or in everyday life. They will happily draw crayon 'pictures' on paper (or on their bedroom walls!), or try to turn a lump of plasticine or playdough into a 'flower' or a 'cake'.

l) **Speed at learning games** Is your child particularly quick at learning games like Dominoes or 'Snap'? (When playing Number Dominoes, the size and clarity of the dots on the blocks affects learning speed.)

m) **Ability with puzzles** By the age of three some children, seem to have developed manipulative abilities and a good appreciation of shape and this is reflected in their ability to put together jigsaw puzzles. At this age, a nine- or 12-piece jigsaw is usually enough, but occasionally a child gifted in this area is able to cope with 30 or more pieces. However, the groups of related concepts in memory for this do not necessarily link or cause an intelligence spill-over to academic work, which is more abstract.

n) **Memory** You can test short-term memory by showing your child three objects, and letting him name them, and then hiding them. After two minutes ask him to name them again. Try this exercise once more with four or more objects if he finds three too easy.

Long-term memory can be tested by asking him to describe things you did together yesterday. My son, John, at five years of age, could remember many things long-term much better than me.

o) **Problem solving** This, as distinct from puzzle solving (e.g. finding a route through a maze), demands prerequisite knowledge.

Example If there are five cows in a field and the giant takes two, how many are left? In order for a child to answer this knowledge of numbers is required.

Even a simple statement like, 'Listen to what I say. In the morning, I get up and get dressed. First I put on my jumper then my shirt, trousers, shoes and lastly my socks,' needs knowledge of dressing order before a child can carry out the task of dressing himself.

Nonsense statements are a good test of problem solving, although a line like, 'The spider ate up the elephant' got no response from one little Asian boy, who eventually asked, 'What's an elephant?'

Statements like, 'The water was so hot that when I put my foot in it, it made me shiver', require considerable conceptual understanding because a three-year-old does not always see the link between shivering and being *cold*. Often the word *shiver* is not properly understood. The relevant age chapters and the tests at the end of the book will provide ideas on problem-solving tests.

Once you have a reasonably good idea of the bodies of knowledge in memory, it will be easier to build concept upon concept and link items already established. Through your questioning, your child will develop groups of related concepts that have deep meaning. The range of these can be developed in a relatively systematic way. For most parents this 'intelligence building' only occupies a small fraction of a child's day. It should be a welcome diversion from undirected play.

Extending meanings by building on concepts that your child understands

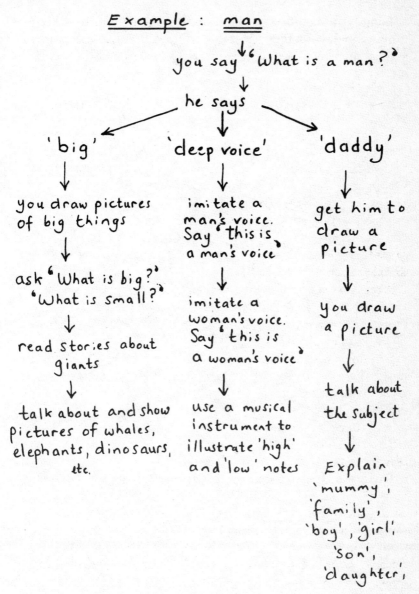

Example : man

you say "What is a man?"

he says

'big' | 'deep voice' | 'daddy'

'big'

you draw pictures of big things

ask "What is big?" "What is small?"

read stories about giants

talk about and show pictures of whales, elephants, dinosaurs, etc.

'deep voice'

imitate a man's voice. Say "this is a man's voice"

imitate a woman's voice. Say "this is a woman's voice"

use a musical instrument to illustrate 'high' and 'low' notes

'daddy'

get him to draw a picture

you draw a picture

talk about the subject

Explain 'mummy', 'family', 'boy', 'girl', 'son', 'daughter', etc.

Talk about concepts through animals

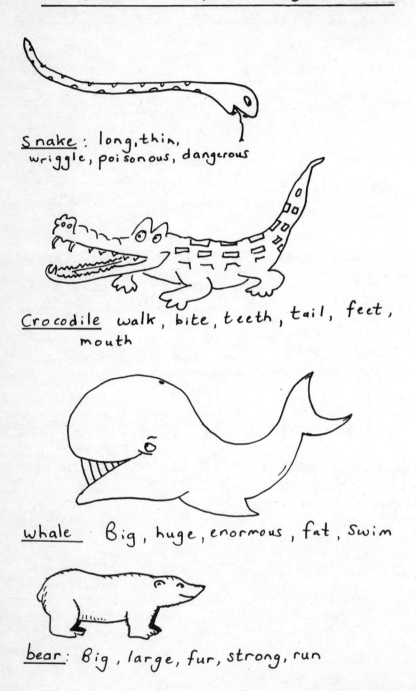

Snake : long, thin, wriggle, poisonous, dangerous

Crocodile walk, bite, teeth, tail, feet, mouth

whale Big, huge, enormous, fat, swim

bear : Big, large, fur, strong, run

<u>parrot</u> Big beak, bird, claws, perch, fly, perch, chatter, talk

<u>dinosaur</u>: horns, big, long ago, no more left

<u>Family</u>

Dad
father
man

Mum
mother
woman
lady

girl
daughter

boy
son

Right and Left Hemispheres

There is an interesting dichotomy in brain structure that may indicate that some linking of related concepts is easier than others. The right hemisphere of the brain deals with primarily non-verbal memory and the emotions, while the left hemisphere is concerned with language, mathematics and abstract thinking in the main. It is important not to neglect one at the expense of the other. It should also be remembered when considering what knowledge to impart to a child, that discipline, or the ability to concentrate, is learnt through activities such as dance, sculpture, painting, drawing, drama and music, as well as the so-called 'academic subjects'. Discipline learnt in association with relaxation and pleasure results in a high level of motivation, learning to dance also links discipline with movement. Maths will not easily link to this discipline association because most of it has no element of mobility.

Reasoning and Thinking

The importance of encouraging reasoning and thinking cannot be underestimated. Very extrovert and sociable children who have played outdoors for much of their young lives and have had little productive conversation with adults, may have bodies of knowledge in memory that represent colloquialisms, such as, 'Have a nice day', copied from other children and adults together with purely manipulative abilities. There may be little development of reasoning and general thinking abilities in such children. Whole bodies of related concepts can be developed at the superficial level because a child has not had recourse to 'looking into things'. Much of such thinking, and certainly academic reasoning ability (as distinct from practical, 'common-sense' reasoning), comes from the attempts to cross-link groups of related concepts in long-term memory. Play, without some thinking that is initiated by environmental influences, will not fulfil the intellectual needs of your child and certainly he will not fulfil his potential. It is important, therefore, to encourage questions on all topics. However, some questions can only encourage a limited answer. Thus:

'What is that?'

'That is a tractor.'

The sorts of questions that develop far-reaching thinking are those that are discussion provoking. For example: 'Why did Jack change the cow for some beans?' asks Tommy, aged four after listening to a fairy tale. And later, 'Why does the giant want to kill Jack?'

When looking at a picture of the Golden Gate Bridge across San Francisco Bay, my son John queries, 'Is it really Gold?' I look into his eyes and they are shining because he is adding dimension to the picture in the book, drawing together aspects of form and depth within his mind and creating a more tangible real-life image to savour. This is done through so-called imagination. Links are made between various items of knowledge in memory to give a sense of 'really being there'. Of course, those bodies of knowledge must already be in memory. You cannot 'draw' on what you do not have.

The exercising of the ability to draw together sometimes widely diverging groups of concepts, is, itself, stored in memory. The new links, themselves, will then create an entirely new meaning, and this is the essence of creativity. The toddler stage is the ideal time to start fostering such a questioning and thinking mentality. Some three-year-olds, of course, need little encouragement in the questioning department!

'Why is this road so long?' asks Simon.

'Because it has to take cars to town – to market,' says Mum.

'Can it be smaller?' he persists.

'Then it won't get to the market, will it?' says Mum.

'They should make it more closer,' says Simon, very positively, 'then we won't have to walk so far.'

A mother's answers to questions are extremely important. Monosyllabic replies do *not* develop reasoning and thinking because it is the active mind searching for possible new meaning that is all-important. A parent needs either to explain fully or to add another question to an answer to extend the discussion.

The toddler phase of continually posing questions is important for resolving conflicts. If you send a child away without a reasonable answer, half-resolved links are left in long-term memory. The child is left 'hanging in a mental vacuum'. The mind may not rest until some solution is found and without a parent's help links may be incorrect. Even if you do not have the solution to his query a link can be created without a definite answer because it links to something that means 'unknown, even by my Mummy'. If your child asks, 'Where do the stars in the sky come from?' you can still say, 'Nobody really knows.'

Words

Words are only important as far as the context is concerned – we skim for meanings – and also when they are in correct meaningful order ('Come over here' rather then 'Here over come'!). This illustrates that though word meanings are of crucial importance, your child also needs practice ranging word order. This comes from intelligent verbal communication and through reading. The subtleties of meanings in written sentences also need to be learnt from reading and from drama. Television drama is useful for teaching a child to read between the lines but the range of word used is limited. Great instructional value for a child of three to six years old can be gained from reading classic stories to him and explaining the twists and turns of the plot and the vagaries of human nature. If a child is subjected to a continuous diet of soaps and simplistic conflict between good and evil then a wide variety of shades of meaning will be lost. A child even of this age is well aware of the subtleties of human emotion and a simplistic treatment of the complexities of human nature will only serve to lead him to distrust his instinct and the understanding gleaned from attempting to manipulate adults.

Opening the Wires

Sometimes both adults and children are immediately aware of the meanings of information. So is that recognition of certain concepts quick because I have 'opened' the wires to the areas including these concepts? For example, if somebody starts to talk about an argument he had with somebody last night, do I immediately open the 'lines' to the related concepts connected to that subject? So if somebody were to suddenly switch from talking about arguments to talking about holidays, it would surely take time to open the wires to this new subject? *Expectation* is, therefore, highly important. If I do not expect the car in front to stop, I am not fully prepared to depress the brakes. Thus learning requires 'priming' your child on a subject so that he is not 'caught cold'. This does not merely involve revising related concepts and elements of those concepts, it concerns an awakening of the routes to the areas of long-term memory that are concerned with the subject you wish to teach.

Problems

Problem solving in a sense is the opposite mental exercise to creative thinking. It is the dissecting of information into essential components or concepts, and then analysing the meaning of the relations between those elements. The approach to problem solving is, itself, stored in memory and the earlier your child can gain confidence in his own ability to solve problems in a logical and systematic way, the more successful he will be in academic life. This confidence comes from the realisation that there are no set answers to many problems and also an enjoyment in his own ability to derive solutions without help.

Incentives to Learning

Many small children do not naturally take to sitting down to solve puzzles or to count buttons. They prefer scooting a plastic car up the driveway, or digging in grandpa's rose-beds. Motivation is, therefore, a powerful weapon in developing concentration, and rewards are particularly important in encouraging your child to sit down and attend to some aspect of learning.

Rewards and Encouragement A three-year-old needs frequent 'rewarding', perhaps as much as every few minutes. However, there are a wide variety of such rewards and some are very basic and fundamental. Here are some ideas:

a) *Social rewards*
  (i)   Contact: A cuddle. A pat on the back. A kiss. A tickle.
  (ii) Expressions: Smile.
  (iii) Speech: 'Good boy/girl.' 'How clever you are!'
  (iv) Attention: Being with your child. Taking notice of his or her comments.

b) *Food or drink* Something to work towards such as a sweet, a biscuit or a drink at the end of a period of time.

c) *Other* The promise of an outing, watching a favourite television programme or video, etc.

Other learning incentives include the use of humour to develop a relaxed atmosphere. This should not go too far, and result in silly behaviour otherwise your child will learn nothing. Simply reading a short, humorous story can often encourage him to take part in what can be termed 'learning play'. However, if he is particularly tired, if interesting visitors have arrived, or a favourite cartoon is on television, teaching periods should be temporarily abandoned.

SUMMARY

What you as a parent will need to do:

a) **Discover knowledge in memory** Discover what bodies of knowledge there are in your child's memory. This knowledge includes all forms of knowledge including such things as manipulative ability and the knowledge of sounds. There are, of course, physical limitations on what a child can do. A child who cannot hold a pencil cannot write.

b) **Introduce new knowledge** Try to decide what knowledge you feel should be linked to existing knowledge. For example, a three-year-old who can draw circles well will be able to copy many letters well. Bear in mind, however, when trying to build on word meanings that simple sounding concepts are, in fact, often quite complex. In memory even a concrete word like *house* would be represented in the following way:

A House

Superficial Meaning   image with no word meanings attached

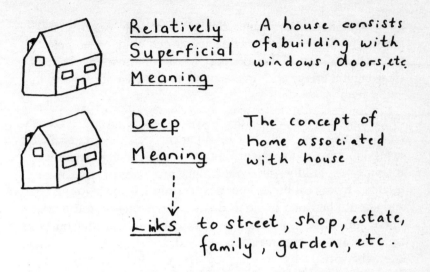

Relatively Superficial Meaning

A house consists of a building with windows, doors, etc

Deep Meaning

The concept of home associated with house

Links to street, shop, estate, family, garden, etc.

These links to other concepts are particularly important to develop as they improve thinking and deepen your child's awareness of particular concepts. A *house*, for example, is often associated with concepts of *home* and *family*.

A child who has never lived in a house, or seen anybody doing so, will not have the prerequisite knowledge in memory for understanding the concept of a house as a *home*. It will merely be a structure with rectangular holes in it. Thus an eskimo child might ask, 'What is a large box doing here? Do I store whale blubber in it? Or can it be used to slide me over the ice chasing polar bears?'

Real-life experience is the most likely knowledge to be able to link to long-term memory and create deep meaning. You will have to give meaning to abstract concepts by linking to concrete experience.

The real-life representation of *sad* is *tears. Miserable* or *upset* could also fit with the picture but very young children do not often use such words.

c) **Present new knowledge clearly** This does not necessarily mean drawing a clear picture, although that often helps. It means ensuring that the concept or facet of knowledge creates a clear mental image and links exactly to the area of memory that you intend it to.

d) **Encourage your child to practise** This will ensure establishment in memory. This can be done through the creation of a mental *picture* and overlearning. Although much practice is not irksome, especially the continuous and almost unconscious learning from real life, some most certainly is for a young child and should be done in small doses over a long period of time. There should be no question of forcing the learning on your child because 'concentration' gained by such methods may, later, be offset by a lack of interest in academic work. Pleasurable associations should be linked to learning sessions.

e) **Help your child to recall.** This is the ability to remember what is already established in memory. If the learning has been linked to real-life experience, or information learnt packaged together in similar-sounding, similar-looking groups, then recall is easier. Older children, up to six years old, benefit from learning spellings in such groups. For example:

bad   mad   sad   had   lad

cat   mat   sat   fat   hat

f) **Create a good environment** The creation of an environment that invites exploration and leads to the development of wide-ranging concepts is important. The later chapters give some ideas about what is needed to create such environments. But you will need to take measures to surround learning by a relaxed atmosphere, by injecting humour into the proceedings or relating the learning in some manner to a child's interest. However, the atmosphere must not detract from learning. Pop music played while a three-year-old is learning to count, for example, may lead him to want to dance, not sit at the table 'playing' with buttons.

g) **Prepare maps of conceptual awareness.** One of the best ways to assess your child's knowledge and further his progress is to prepare maps or charts of conceptual awareness. This can be extremely laborious but is worthwhile in the long run. Such a map can be illustrated by reference to the word 'window'. The following illustrates what a three-year-old's memory may have stored:

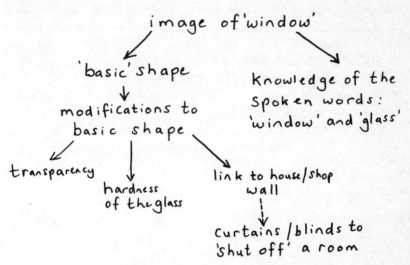

You will notice that this knowledge is almost entirely of the real-world, 'hands-on' variety. What you will need to link to this experience is mostly so-called 'abstract' knowledge thus developing greater conceptual awareness in your child.

Spoken words

break / smash
↓
pieces / bits
↓
sharp
↓
hurt
↓
danger
↓
written words of the same group of concepts

As you introduce knowledge in a systematic way there will be easy linkage to memory and easy recall of items. It is most effective, in other words, to concentrate on teaching *within* a body of knowledge, as indicated above. If you follow this advice your child's progress can be spectacular. However, many children show only slow or sporadic intellectual development until at some point an 'explosion' of intelligence occurs. It is as if a thousand tentative linkages to memory suddenly become established, resulting in a bound forward intellectually. Whichever path your child takes, he will be better prepared for school, confident and highly motivated.

Tests for all the age groups are set out at the end of the book on pages 132–150 as well as the suggestions mentioned in each chapter.

CHAPTER FOUR

YOUR CHILD AT THREE

Three-year-olds are often full of burgeoning ideas and questions.

'I like elephants,' said Josi.

'Why?' I asked.

'Because they is big,' she said. 'If I was big I wouldn't be little.'

'I know,' I said.

'Then people would see me,' she said.

Children of this age will ask, 'What is this?' They also talk to themselves, to their teddies or in play. They are beginning to play alongside other children but they are still often solitary.

Your child is an actor, loving to dress up in second-hand clothes or anything she can get hold of especially cast-off clothes. Acting adds deeper meaning to much of the behaviour she observes in life. She use sentences but often strings together short ones experimentally. She is often unsure of herself, asking frequently, 'Is that right?' But by now she is beginning to cooperate.

A three-year-old's grammar is quite complex already and they often have a 1,000-word vocabulary. They can run, turn corners, ride a tricycle, stand on one foot, cut with scissors (although to hold paper and scissors at the same time is a trial), and match jigsaw shapes in a 12-piece jigsaw. She likes to use crayons and can copy a cross and a circle:

Nikita, aged 3½

She can draw a representation of a man where the head and body are merged into one (*see* page 75 for more about this).

Your child often knows colours at this age but for those who do not know the *meaning* of colour, you will need to point out different objects of the same colour in the house, in the street or garden. She can fold a rectangular piece of paper, but not obliquely. She can undo buttons and take off clothes and shoes. She will sit at the table to work and be bargained with.

There are 'disequilibrium' and 'equilibrium' ages between three and five although the age categories are not strict ones. They represent the average for an age group only. In disequilibrium, nothing pleases, but your child is not your enemy. It is not you against her, merely the result of a development of spirit and an accompanying non-conformist spirit.

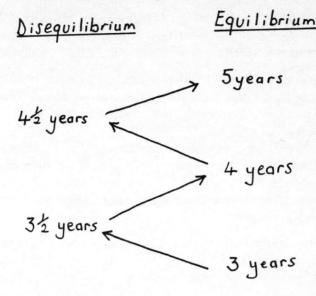

Nursery Schools

At three your child may well be ready for nursery school. There are many nursery schools to which you can send your child, both council and privately owned. Some of these are excellent and some are not. When you have looked at local nursery education using the following criteria, ask yourself if you could not do better at home yourself. The following is a list of things to watch out for at a nursery school:

a) It should have a wide range of practical materials to investigate mathematical and scientific concepts through discovery (e.g. sand, water, building blocks, weighing scales). Clear objectives should be set. Nothing is so soul destroying for a child as to be given material and be asked, 'Find out something'.

b) The school should ensure that abstract concepts are introduced steadily, in clearly defined stages, building on real-life knowledge in memory and using concrete material.

c) There should be other practical experience to teach a wide range of manipulative skills e.g. home skills, dressing, undressing, tying laces, running, hopping, skipping, swimming.

d) There should be an atmosphere in which teachers talk to children, explaining meanings through concrete examples and pictures, discussing their work and encouraging them.

e) *Pre-reading*. There should also be clear labelling of objects, the use of pictures for discussion in groups or individually. The reading of nursery rhymes, jingles and stories should be illustrated dramatically or pictorially.
Reading There should be a clear attempt to introduce the abstract symbols of written words through multifarious methods including phonics, 'Look and Say', reading along with children, and through the use of all the senses. A good library is essential.

f) There should be both materials and opportunities to develop creative potential in Art, Craft, Drama and Music, with perhaps the chance to learn to play a musical instrument.

g) There should be a wide range of games to develop facets of intelligence, e.g. dominoes, draughts, chess.

h) Children should be introduced to the computer and calculator preferably through simple educational games and be informed through educational material on television, radio, videos, cassettes and disks.

i) There should be consideration of the personality and needs of the individual and an attempt to foster confidence and interest in the academic. A system of 'rewards' is preferable.

j) A system of assessment should be in place to determine what a child knows at various ages.

Montessori Nursery Schools Some of the aims expressed above are embraced by Montessori schools, but many are not. Exploration and discovery are present in these nursery schools and there is much emphasis on harmony and cooperation. However, there is less reception learning, when knowledge is given to a child through the medium of a teacher. There is no competitive atmosphere in a true Montessori environment so there are no rewards or punishments. The directress (as opposed to teacher) guides rather than informs. There is certainly emphasis on concrete experiences for the child and attempts to link with abstract symbols but often these efforts will not result in a child well advanced enough in this respect to be successful and confident in my view in a normal State infant school. However, if you send your child to most private schools at the age of four, a year before entry into State schools, this will advance their understanding of abstract symbols. This is the ideal situation for a young child who has attended a Montessori school and should result in a highly motivated and bright child.

TALKING

Pre-school children verbalise out loud on their own to ensure that they remember what they have to do and to establish the order of doing those activities ('I will do this, then I do that . . .). They also talk to themselves in play, acting a part in role-play, practising and testing meanings, creating mental pictures in their minds to facilitate concentration. However, it is through older brothers and sisters and in particular parents that the widest variety of meanings are learnt. If parents do not concern themselves consciously with explanation, then it is very likely that their child will become disadvantaged in an academic sense. Even simple spoken sentences involve the use of many highly abstract concepts; it is only through verbal intercourse with adults that children form an appreciation of the deeper meanings of not only words but the relationships between words and phrases and associated inferences. It is the word, both spoken and written, that enables the concept to be crystallised and thus advances thought.

However, it is extremely difficult to teach concepts (e.g. 'this is a tree') directly. They can only be built up slowly and over a period of time and by linking to experience already in memory. It is not enough simply to explain: your child needs to see a tree, to feel the leaves, to collect conkers. An appreciation of form and patterns which is the essence of perception can then be linked to this particular form and the variations of that form. Also, some appreciation of the fact that a tree is alive may be gained from planting a sapling in the back garden and noting its growth after a year, and then relating that growth to that of cress seedlings.

It would be a parent's job to point out a wide variety of 'trees', without naming individual forms, and the characteristics of 'tree' (branch, trunk, leaf, tall, straight, roots, growing, etc.). Some concepts attached to the idea of 'tree' are difficult to pursue in normal circumstances: for example, a tree transpires, transports food and water, reproduces, photosynthesises. To try to explain such ideas to a pre-school child would result in little more than rote learning. Schoolwork demands only a basic conceptual understanding and *this* is what a parent needs to aim at in her child. But the importance of talking to your child cannot be emphasized too much. So at this stage you should talk about concrete things at home. Here are some ideas:

Object Name	Associated Words
table	top, legs, wood, eat, food
chair	sit, soft, hard
door	in, out, handle, close, open
bed	covers, duvet, sleep, warm
fire	hot, flame, electric, gas
window	glass, smash, look through, outside, inside
bath	water, empty, full, float, sink, bubbles, soap, wash, clean, dirty
kitchen	cooker, cupboard, knives, forks, spoons, plates, fridge (cool), saucepan
garden	tree, grass, shed, garage, path, flowers, bush
person	eye, ear, head, hand, arm, nose, mouth, finger, foot, leg, tummy, lips, hair, see, hear, touch, taste, smell, walk, run, sit
town	bus, car, shop, train, station, school, office, lamp-post, street

In each environment point out concrete objects and, if she is very familiar with them, bring in associated words. Thus:

'What do you call this?'
'A window.'

'If you hit it too hard it will smash and you will fall outside.'

'What's smash?'

'It means that the window will break up into tiny, sharp pieces that can cut you. A window is there so that you can look through it to see the garden and also it lets the light in.'

I have already written about this in the previous chapter but such a conversation does begin to build links in a child's mind, and I stress that it needs to be repeated fairly frequently in order to cement the new knowledge in memory. Associating abstract words with concrete words (e.g. to 'smash' or 'break' a window) is a good way to communicate understanding of difficult concepts. As you talk to your child she will also unconsciously learn further sentence structure.

By talking about incidents in stories you can also explain words, discuss inferences and teach comprehension in general. The important thing is not to be worried by repetition when talking to your child. Children love the repetition of stories, rhymes, jingles and of words in general. Pictures help to cement information in memory, so the talking is best done around a picture or a video film. A film like *Snow White and the Seven Dwarfs*, for example, can introduce a child in a very meaningful way to concepts such as pride, jealousy and anger. Even the names of the dwarfs and their behaviour teach the meanings of emotions – Grumpy, Bashful, Sleepy, etc. Your child may forget a word, but probably never the behaviour of the Wicked Queen and her words, 'Mirror, mirror on the wall, who is the fairest one of all?' Embraced in such a scene are inferences of jealousy and vanity, which can be explained to a pre-school child in simple words: 'The Wicked Queen wants to be the most beautiful lady in the world.' And, 'Now she is cross because Snow White is prettier. See how terribly angry and cruel that makes her.' This is an area in which many adults could take a lesson: understanding the motivations behind actions is a lost art.

Musical accompaniment also makes an experience more memorable. So binding knowledge into memory.

Concrete Word Meanings

A picture tells a story. The simple picture of a *mouth* links with sucking, eating, biting, licking, kissing, tasting, and also with other concrete objects on the face such as skin, nose, chin, etc. A child does not always create a clear picture in her mind of each of these meanings, but the vaguer mental images will be there. A simple question like, 'What does a mouth do?' will often lead a child to create clear mental pictures and put into words the linked meanings.

Below are some useful concrete words with pictures that you can talk about to your three-year-old. There is, of course, no need, at this stage, to attempt to teach reading, although some children will learn to read the words incidentally anyway.

face

body

trousers

jumper

sock

skirt

dog

cat

elephant

horse

banana

apple

egg

cakes

ball

hand

doll

boy

girl

policeman

house

sun

door

cup

spoon

car

television

tree

ship (boat)

bus

train

bread

chair

Talk about concepts through animals

<u>Swan</u>: long neck, beak, wing, float, glide, graceful, feathers, bird, paddle

<u>penguin</u>: walk, not fly, fish, waddle, swim, feathers, bird, snow, ice

<u>monkey</u>: climb, swing, jump, tail, fur, chatter, trees, jungle

<u>giraffe</u>: tall, high, look down, walk, stand

Abstract Word Meanings

Your child, at three, will have little knowledge of abstract meanings. Some of the following you may have to explain carefully.

Brick Building

Many word meanings can be explained in play with a variety of shapes. For more on shapes *see* later in this chapter.

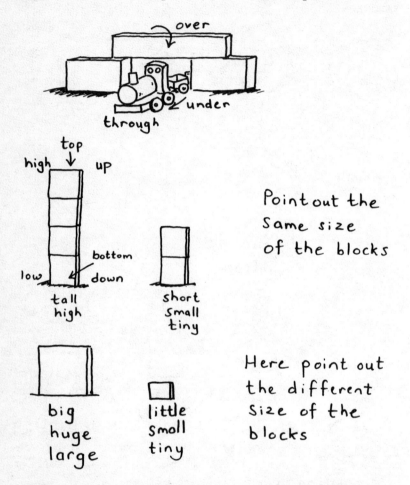

Point out the same size of the blocks

Here point out the different size of the blocks

Other word meanings that can be explained include: big, bigger, biggest; small, smaller, smallest; long, longer, longest. (Straws can also be used to illustrate this by cutting them to different sizes.)

the middle one

Your child will need practice for this concept to be fully learnt. Initially, a middle one that is different emphasises the idea, but a child will need to appreciate that a middle one can have the same shape, colour and size of those surrounding it. Also he should realise that there is only a middle one of any odd number in a line.

READING

Books

The most important association that a child must gain from reading is pleasure. You can build this in your child's mind by sitting her on your knee and reading a picture book to her, talking about the pictures and answering questions as you go along. You must read the story with expression and trace the words with your finger showing her that the sentences run from left to right. Children from a young age are thrilled and relaxed by nursery rhymes and stories read to them at bed-time, in particular. The association of, here, a loving relationship with mother and reading, is important, because memories established at this age will last throughout life.

Many word meanings can be taught, incidentally, and your child can learn to read 'between the lines', finding out how people (and animal-people) behave. Acting out the story, of course, strengthens links in memory.

'Look! The giant is this big!' I said to John, drawing myself up to my full height and standing on a chair. His eyes opened with wonder.

'And,' I said, 'he talks like this.' Deepening my voice and talking louder, 'Fee-Fi-Fo-Fum!'. Soon, he was copying me when he could read: 'And Red Riding Hood said, "What big teeth you've got, Grandma!"'

The knowledge of the 'form' of a story, the pattern of its presentation, is also retained in memory and this is valuable experience for school English later. Stories also illustrate opposites. For example:

Giant – large, huge, big
Jack – small, tiny, little
Wicked Queen – bad, evil, cruel, nasty
Snow White – kind, good

As you read along point out colours, count when you can and take every opportunity to mention the names of concrete objects. Remember, also, that your child likes repetition. This is mainly due to the mind's need to learn things and part of her drive to acquire knowledge in order to ensure survival. So repeat, repeat, repeat. It will give her a sense of *security* by enhancing information in memory; unanswered questions make for insecurity through life. Not knowing in a particular environment puts a child at a disadvantage and heavily reliant on others for guidance.

You will find a list of suitable picture books, poetry, rhymes and fairy stories on pages 157–162

The Beginning of Learning to Read

From the onset it is important to realise that if two children had exactly the same background, one would still learn to read quicker than the other. Some children have that mysterious ability to take in, absorb and cement information effortlessly. This is an ability to separate from input the essential core information and create a clear mental *picture* (as opposed to a fleeting, indistinct mental image), whether of something abstract (like an idea) or of something concrete. Children can be taught to some extent to do this but a gifted few are able to do so from a very young age.

Naming Cards

When your child is aware of the names of things around the house it is a useful beginning to learning to read to *label* those objects using 7 × 7cm (3 × 3in) white card.

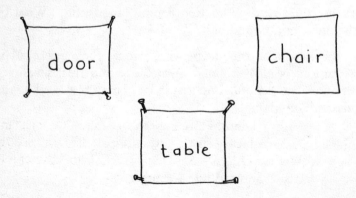

Grouping labelled objects together contributes to overlearning by feeding the mind with similar sounding and looking syllables. Label soft toys and objects such as:

cat
rat
mat
hat

It is difficult to find a profusion of objects with similar letter strings. You will simply have to make best use of what you have. Some play sets, like those from Duplo, include farm and zoo sets to extend the possibility of labelling. Labelling toys is an excellent way of connecting reading with the outside world. The attempt to make the subject more concrete forges links in memory, creates clear mental pictures that have deep meaning, and contributes to overlearning.

The Alphabet
The letters themselves do not have particular significance at this stage. However, your child will enjoy learning the letters in a sing-song way. Use lower-case letters when tracing with the tune:

a b c d e f g h i j k l m n
o p q r s t u v w x y z

Later, capital letters can be introduced and she will be able to recognise them on road signs and shop fronts:

A B C D E F G H I J K L M N
O P Q R S T U V W X Y Z

Reading Cards
The next stage in reading is pasting a picture on card and writing its name above or below. Letters should be written large (though not enormous) because then they capture the child's attention and a clear image is produced.

You will notice that the above are all nouns and, initially, in reading, certain key words that occur up to 1,000 times more often than nouns in text are better learnt. Unfortunately, these are also difficult to relate to real life to create clear mental pictures and facilitate learning. The deep meaning of words like 'the' (*definite* article) and 'a' (*indefinite* article) are best avoided at this stage. An emphasis on shape and sound is better, tracing the word shape in a sand tray and making up the words with 'solid' letters.

Key Words

First group

a   and   he   I   in   is   it   of   that   the   to   was

A useful technique that seems to fix concentration is to write a word fairly small on some card and then to write the same word, bigger and bigger, on successive cards. Place the words in a pile, smallest on top to biggest on the bottom and read them with your child one after the other.

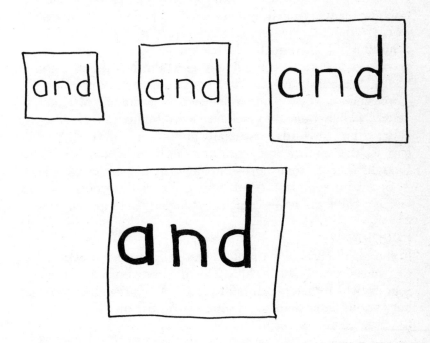

Second group

all   as   at   be   but   are   for   had   have   him   his

not   on   one   said   so   they   we   with   you

A Reading Scheme

There is a modern trend to abandon reading schemes in favour of 'read-along' methods which use ungraded books. The reasons for using such methods are to encourage fluency and to keep a child's interest in books alive. However, these methods tend to be slower than Look and Say methods, where there is greater repetition of words. The aim, initially, should be the fostering of confidence, and in spite of the stilted nature of some reading-scheme texts, most pre-school children learn to read quickly. Interest is fostered through that confidence, good presentation and colourful pictures, and other factors like parental attention and approval. Ladybird Books produce a good Key Words scheme that is cheap and readily available through bookshops. Their series of fairy stories is especially liked by small children.

A strong objection to picking up *any* reading book and to teaching reading from it, is that there is not enough repetition of words in the early stages. Learning to read is best done through a multifarious use of methods: reading along with your child to encourage fluency, encouraging interest through use of picture books, 'look and say' with key words to teach recognition of word shape and promote confidence, and the use of phonics (letter/syllable sounds) to facilitate word building.

Repetition of words is especially important in the early stages because the reading of a word not followed by another fairly soon displaces it from short-term memory. In many books there is an over-preponderance of nouns, especially proper nouns, which a child will never come across again (e.g. kipper).

Phonics

In the early stages of learning to read it is sensible practice not to over-burden a small child with the rote learning of letter sounds, which then becomes drudgery. As you read text, point out various letter shapes and sounds, without dwelling on them too much. For example:

S like a snake – s-s-s-s-s-s

C curly C – cat

K kicking K –

A complete phonics list is given in the next chapter but if your child learns to read very quickly start to use this list, together with word building, at an earlier stage. There is a large number of children who, by three, are for one reason or another, very ready to learn to read.

Whatever learning activities your child is taking part in, it is made more effective by asking her to close her eyes and visualise a word or an activity. Sometimes she may be able to visualise against the backdrop of a bare wall. In effect, the 'rehearsal', as it may be called, is practice, and that creation of a mental picture is reinforcement of the meaning of an experience.

WRITING

Writing will eventually become one of the main elements of output, that is, activities that cement new experience in memory and forge new links between related concepts.

Three is a good age to begin to show your child how to draw certain shapes.

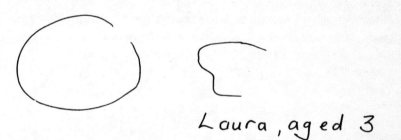

Letters o or c are the first shapes to attempt, although children vary in their ability to draw these at first.

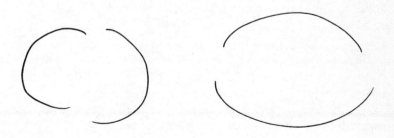

Another letter that can be attempted at this stage is l. Get your child to draw patterns on large sheets of sugar paper using crayon.

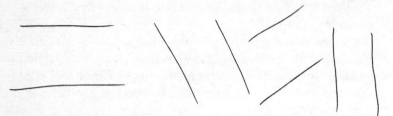

Tracing round dots is also very popular with very young children. Practise repeating the same letter.

Some children are particularly ready, in a physical sense, to begin writing. Others need prerequisite practice. Extend the pattern-making as soon as your child shows interest and capability. Here are some examples of how to do this:

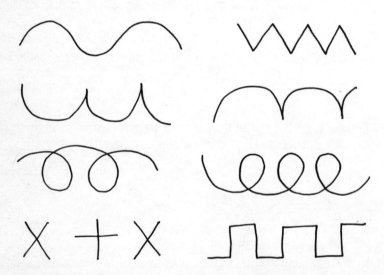

Try including letters periodically but make writing sessions short. Children weary of this activity very quickly.

NUMBER SKILLS

Sorting

This is an important activity if only to ensure that prerequisite concepts are clear in your child's mind. It helps a child to recognise differences in shape, size and colour. Also it may aid her in recognising 'several of a kind', something of importance in counting.

Sort for colour

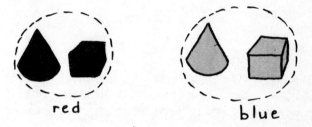

Concentrate on one colour at a time. Explain the primary colours first: red, blue and yellow. Then secondary colours such as green, orange, purple. A knowledge of white, black, grey and pink is also useful in real life. Shades of colours cause considerable confusion at first. The tape 'Yellow Submarine' from the Early Learning Centre is helpful when learning about colours.

Sort for shape

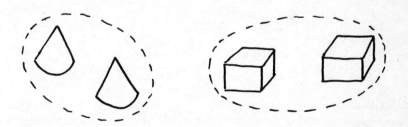

Use these words when sorting for shape: different, same, shape, corner, curves. Place the four shapes on a table and show your child how to sort for shape. Then ask her to do this on her own.

Sort for size

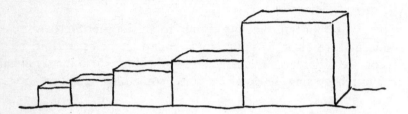

Make a 'train' then use these words to help sort for size: big, little, tall, short, small, order.

Order Sorting Activities

Your child can sort out a small pile of socks, clothes for various people, toys for size, colour or shape, coins in order of size, and sticky paper shapes can be used as an alternative to the 'flat' shapes used above.

Ordering

Show your child how to alternate shapes, mix them up and then ask her to put them in order. You can use these associated words: order, next, after.

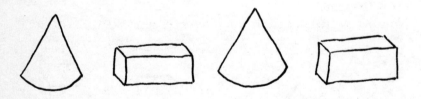

Matching

This activity includes matching like with like, particularly in games such as 'Snap'. You can draw many variations on the following themes.

Get your child to draw lines between the pictures that are the same:

Now get her to spot the three differences in these two pictures:

Pairing

This involves putting items into related groups. For example, knives with forks, cups with saucers. 'Happy Families' is a game that develops this skill.

Ask your child to draw lines between the things that go together.

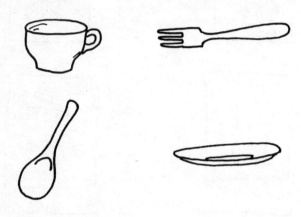

Problems and Puzzles

Puzzle-solving represents fairly superficial processes in learning whereas problem-solving both tests and teaches deeper meaning and is, in effect, an investigation into concepts. A jigsaw puzzle tests a child's ability to recognise and match shapes, whereas a problem asking, 'What is wrong with these pictures?' requires the child to know that a man (generally) has two arms and two legs, an aircraft two wings and a car has four wheels.

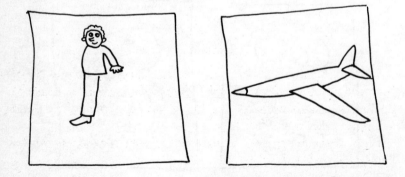

A child will need to know that a tree does not hang upside down in the air:

The image created by an incomplete object will have a 'match' with the generalised representation of it in memory, and the missing part should be recognised immediately. However, recognition will depend on what knowledge is in memory. By drawing pictures with parts missing, or in impossible situations, your child's conceptual understanding can be assessed. Choose concepts like tree, house, street, garden, car, boat, train, door, window, table, chair, or bed. Each concept depends on subsidiary, prerequisite concepts. For example, it is impossible to know what a bed is without the knowledge of sleep in memory.

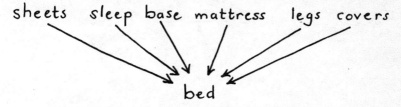

In real-life situations you can stretch your child's powers of reasoning by presenting her with the wrong end of the brush to do her hair with or by giving her a jumper upside down and asking, 'Is this right?'

Push your son's toy car along upside down and ask, 'Is there a better way to do this?'

Humour not only relaxes, it can serve a more subtle purpose. Humorous conversation probes the depths of conceptual understanding. An adult stating the ridiculous creates an image that conflicts with what a child *knows* is the true state of affairs. If she does not know she will not react in the appropriate way. The following illustrates the point when the child does know the true state of affairs:

'Why,' I said to Hannah, 'am I so little and you so big?'

The three-year-old collapsed into gales of laughter. 'Don't be silly,' she said, 'I am little. You are big.'

'But look,' I continued, sinking low in my armchair, 'I am littler than you. You are a giant, I am so small.'

Again there were gales of laughter.

'Look,' she said, 'you are a Daddy. I am just a little girl.'

'Why,' I said, wide-eyed 'aren't you married?'

Investigating Shapes

A good set of children's bricks is excellent for the investigation of shape. Ideally it would need to include 'flat' solid bricks to represent two-dimensional shapes. At this stage the names of the shapes are not important but the link to real life is.

Point out to your child the presence of the shapes in real life. Here are some obvious examples:

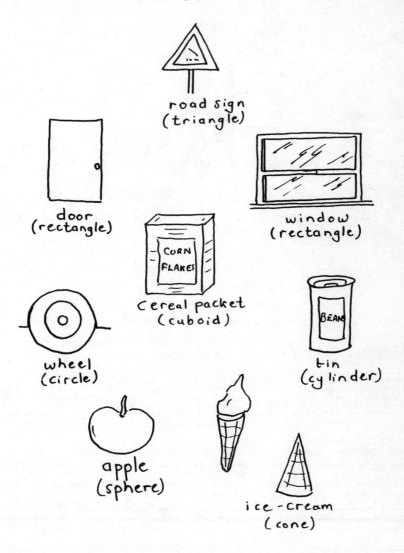

road sign
(triangle)

door
(rectangle)

window
(rectangle)

cereal packet
(cuboid)

wheel
(circle)

tin
(cylinder)

apple
(sphere)

ice-cream
(cone)

Opposites

The emphasising of opposites creates a clear mental image in a child's mind and, therefore, the meaning of the words.

Actions and music create a more memorable mental image and establish firm links.

Inside, outside, upside, down,
Round about and up the town.
Clap your hands and stamp your feet,
Squirm about upon the seat.

Counting

Real-life objects are best for learning counting, and one of the best exercises is counting the stairs up to bed. The *feel* of the step at each count serves to add dimension and image to the *sound* of the count and the *sight* of the successive steps.

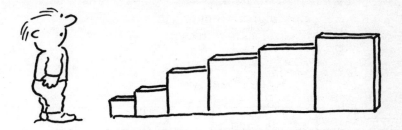

At first count only 1–2–3; later 1–2–3–4–5. You can reinforce the link to memory by counting houses along the street, *parked* cars (moving cars may produce a confused mental image), and reciting counting rhymes while counting buttons with your child at the table:

When counting objects (sweets, buttons, marbles etc.) it is essential for you to *touch* the items on each count. Better still, it adds depth in a child's mind to get *her* to touch on each count.

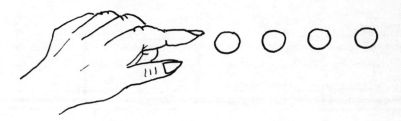

All good children, count together.
One, two, three, four, five.
All good children count together.
One, two, three, four, five.
One, two, three, four, five.
We're glad we are alive.
All good children count together.
One, two, three, four, five.

Children's bricks are also good for counting with. Building a tower, in particular, as the count proceeds creates a sustained image that facilitates memorability:

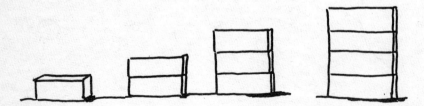

Drawing pictures is an excellent way of teaching your child to count:

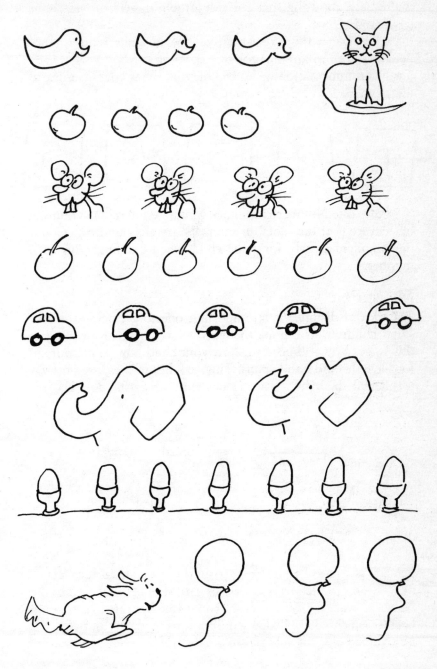

Finally, a good *abacus* or bead frame is very helpful when teaching a pre-school child. For older children a 10 × 10 abacus is the best. By using such an aid, large numbers can easily be envisaged.

Quite often a three-year-old likes to know the written numbers and even to attempt copying them on cards 7 × 7cm (3 × 3in). This information will then link with the deeper meaning of one, two . . .

Games like Number Dominoes stimulate interest in counting but ensure that the 'dots' or numbers are clear and big. Count the numbers clearly for your child placing a finger on each number.

Measuring

The idea of distance is an important one to get across to very small children. The units themselves have no real meaning at this stage. You will need to show your child how to measure in foot-lengths and hand-spans. Then ask her to measure how far it is across the living room. Count with her as she does it.

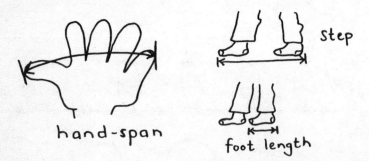

Now is a good time to start marking her height, in centimetres, on a wallchart or a strip of card simply sellotaped to the bedroom wall. As she grows she can watch her rate of growth in height and this knowledge will link into memory. Initially, the unit value will probably not make the link.

INVESTIGATIONS THROUGH PLAY

Three-year-olds have a thirst for knowledge. In the main they wish to know *how* things work – they fiddle with household appliances, their fingers are into everything, driving mothers to distraction. Knowing how is important for survival in a particular environment: I press a button and this happens, I pull down on the door handle and the door opens, and, in more primitive societies, I learn how to fire a bow-and-arrow and hunt for food. There is much joy and satisfaction in learning how to do things – how to run, jump, slide, skip, ride a trike. Academic work, however, demands much more. It requires a child to know that electricity powers household appliances and that it is dangerous, that a tree is a living organism that respires and creates organic food. So, when you teach your child do not confine yourself to giving a name to something and explaining how it works (although related concepts representing such superficial meanings are extremely important). You will need to emphasise the conceptual aspect of words. You can do this by explaining that *tree* needs water from the ground and also sunlight in order to grow and to make its own food from its leaves.

Bearing this in mind, your child will find much to interest her and can re-create the experiences, either in concrete or imaginative play. The words and numbers that you use to qualify those experiences she will use later to communicate her knowledge and understanding in school life. There are many ways in which your child can investigate through play. Listed below are some ideas for you both to investigate.

(1) *In the sink or bath* Water is cold, warm or hot. Some objects float and others sink, some soak up the water and become soggy. Playing with water can lead to an investigation of materials or an appreciation of the power of water to move things. Simply turning on the tap and washing something down the plug-hole illustrates this fact. Free play with water is pleasant for a child but ultimately not of great value educationally. It needs you, the parent, to point out specific things, although this should never become a long, boring instruction session. Your child will do best if one thing at a time is pointed out and

then she is left to investigate. 'This floats and this sinks', illustrates an investigation that could take up many bath-time sessions.

Another activity that fascinates is filling up a container and transferring water to another different-sized container. Plastic cups, of the type babies play with, are very useful, and such investigation into capacity can be helpful later when playing with sand. There is no need to labour over units at this stage or to explain volume in depth. It is enough that the knowledge of quantity is in the memory so that future concepts can be built on it.

(2) *With materials of various textures*   Many word meanings can be learnt when a child is provided with a wide variety of materials to investigate. Apart from sand and water which 'run' through the fingers and change shape with the container they fill, you can ask your child to feel materials like cloth, wood, metal, stone, plastic, plasticine or playdough. You can supply the words that are required to describe the experiences: hard, soft, smooth, rough, shiny, squash, sharp, bend, round, straight, heavy, light. There are comparisons that can also be made between the different textures. 'This is softer than this.' 'That is lighter than that.'

(3) *Growth*   Your child will be thrilled to follow the growth of mustard and cress seeds placed in a plastic egg container on dampened pieces of paper towelling. She will also enjoy tracing the growth of annuals planted in the garden in early summer.

(4) *In the garden*   There is a lot to be learnt from a back garden. Many collections of animals, plants and inanimate objects can be found by a foraging three-year-old. Here are some suggestions: acorns, cones, grass, stones, earth, earth worms, caterpillars, sticks, leaves, fruit.

There are other things but it should be pointed out they are not to be brought inside and some not touched – bees, ants, beetles, grasshoppers, trees, bushes, frogs, slugs, wasps.

Once the curiosity of a three-year-old has been stimulated, it will be difficult to stop her bringing half the garden into the house. When she does bring in the results of her investigations, though, your clear explanations are particularly important. For example:

'What is this, Mummy?' asked Mark.

'It's a caterpillar,' replied his mother.

'What's it for?'

'That little thing will roll itself up into its bed on a leaf and change into a butterfly one day.'

'Why does it do that?'

'Because then it can lay eggs on the leaves to make more caterpillars.'

'Caterpillars is best,' said Mark

'Why?'

'Because they tickle,' said Mark, as the caterpillar climbed over the back of his hand. This demonstrates only too well that a parent also has to deal with the faultless logic of a small child.

(5) *Air*   Illustrate that air has pressure by demonstrating that it can hold up a parachute. Explain that wind is air blowing leaves or your hair about. Blowing through a straw can show your child how this force can be concentrated. Tell her that wind instruments use air pressure to make notes.

Making a parachute can show how air supports weight

parachute

(6) *Dressing up, acting, dancing* You can find old hats, dresses, coats, shoes and other objects at jumble sales to satisfy your child's desire to dress up and re-enact real-life and television situations. Such role play is important to the learning process, satisfying as it does a desire to give deep meaning to observed emotions and to develop links between concepts that are creative. As a parent your discussion of soap operas on television, of films and stories will be the spur to such play. The following example shows how a young girl called Tanya reacts to the witch in the film, *The Wizard of Oz*.

'I don't like that witch,' said Tanya.

'She's green to make her look nasty,' I said.

'Will she come and get me?'

'Of course not. Witches aren't real. It's just in the story.'

'If she comes I'll send Bob [the dog] to get her.'

'That's right.'

'Bob doesn't like that witch.'

'Probably not.'

'He chases witches into the park and they fall in the river.'

Already Tanya had created a story and a dramatic situation to rid herself of her fear. When the witch had fallen into the water in her mind, she felt secure.

There are many play kits available today and young children especially love dressing up as doctors and nurses. Post Office shops complete with till and play money, cash registers with card wipes, play kitchens and tool kits all provide opportunities for role playing and exploring experiences freely.

Small children like to dance. Even baby Tiffany at the age of three months sways to a song I sing to her. At two years of age John would climb onto the dining-room table and dance to children's songs and pop music. There seems to be a clear inheritance factor here; some children have a superior talent for movement that cannot be explained only in terms of what has been learnt. However, all children should be encouraged to dance in time to a wide range of music. Such activity develops coordination as well as providing pure enjoyment and an outlet for natural exuberance particularly on a rainy day.

MUSIC

Children at this stage take great delight in singing along with nursery rhymes and songs. There are many nursery rhymes to choose from but here are some of the most popular:

'Baa, Baa, Black Sheep' 'Ding-Dong Bell' 'Here we go round the Mulberry Bush' 'Hey, Diddle, Diddle' 'Hickory, Dickory Dock' 'Hot Cross Buns' 'Humpty-Dumpty' 'Incey Wincey Spider' 'Jack and Jill' 'Oranges and Lemons' 'Pop! Goes the Weasel' 'See-Saw, Margery Daw' 'Three Blind Mice' 'Twinkle, Twinkle'

Other songs to consider include (*see* also pages 158–162):

'Away in a Manger' 'The animals went in two by two' 'If You're Happy' 'I'm a little tea-pot' 'Jimmy Crack Corn' 'Jingle Bells' 'Li'l Liza Jane' 'Looby-Loo' 'Michael Finnigan' 'Rudolph the Red Nosed Reindeer' 'Silent Night' 'There were ten in a bed' 'Yellow Submarine' 'The Wheels on the Bus'

I'm a little tea-pot

I'm a little tea-pot short and stout
Here's my handle, here's my spout
When it comes to tea-time
Hear me shout
Tip me up and pour me out

Incey, Wincey Spider

Incey, Wincey Spider
Climbing up the spout

Down came the rain
And washed the spider out

Out came the sun
And dried up all the rain

Incey, Wincey Spider
Climbing up again

Clapping hands and stamping feet in rhythm in many of these 'action' songs encourages a sense of timing in a child. Very often when playing a cassette or record a three-year-old will get up and dance.

There are many songs in Walt Disney cartoons, other animated films and story tapes. The combination of animation and song is remembered long after pre-school age. My three- and four-year-olds watched *The Wizard of Oz* at least a hundred times within a year.

You can help your child to beat time to music by using percussion instruments at this age. You can make many of these at home by improvising them. Here are some ideas:

Shakers
a match-box
plastic bottle
tin
threaded milk bottle tops on a string
other containers filled with beans, buttons, rice, or pasta

Drumming Your child can drum various containers with a metal or wooden spoon:
saucepan
plastic bucket
plastic bowl
coke tins
ground coffee tins
ice-cream containers
cake tins

Other ideas could include making chiming instruments and scrapers.

Your child can also begin to learn to play a musical instrument. There are traditional methods which can be very effective and others like the Suzuki method.

The Suzuki method   In the U.K. the Suzuki Institute has undertaken the training of about 150 teachers. Children start learning an instrument at the age of three but parents must become actively involved too. A child listens, first hearing the musical language, and learns in much the same way as she learns her own language. Each new skill is built up gradually and by much repetition and the order of learning skills is extremely important. In addition, the environment for learning is a nurturing one developing the relationship with the parent and fostering confidence.

Starting to play an instrument early helps to develop perfect pitch and teaches a sense of discipline. My own son learnt to play the piano at three by more traditional methods and was one of the youngest to take and pass the London School of Music examination.

ART AND CREATIVE PLAY

A three-year-old is probably very adept at using a short, thick crayon for drawing on sugar paper. The drawing below illustrates this beautifully.

Benjamin
aged 3

Children of this age have detailed related concepts of facial features. A person is a face until they have linked a person to bodily movements, when they will draw the face with arms and legs coming from it. It is not that they cannot recognise a person as head and body, but that they *see* in their mind's eye only the face. The links between body and facial related concepts are not yet firmly established. The question is, should we, as parents, show the link between related concepts, thus 'advancing' our child's artistic impression? Or, should the child 'express' her feelings through art, thus reflecting her state of mind at that period of time? A child of three *sees* a man with a face and body but relates only to the facial part of the man. Therefore, she draws what she feels. In drawing, there are two representations of a man, one an exact or near-exact copy of his form and the other the impressionist representation of our inner view of him.

This could mean that we, as adults, have learnt somewhere along the line to eradicate from our drawings much of the view of a person as seen through a feelingful relationship. A preschool child's view might reflect that aspect more nearly; perhaps our inner view of a person is mostly face, some body and other parts (according to the level of sexual development), and this viewpoint will vary with mood and from one moment to another.

You can, as a parent, see art as an outlet for the expression of feelings – a safety valve if you like. In that case there will be no need to teach your child to copy exactly. However, other aspects of academic work demand the ability to copy: two-dimensional shapes for Maths, animal and body forms for Science. This conflict between the demands of art on the one hand, and other disciplines on the other, is difficult to resolve. Once related concepts have been established that represent a man as a biological unit, it may be difficult for a child to free herself from this in order to express her feelings, which might result in a disproportionate drawing of the man.

Creative Activities

Below is a list of activities and materials a parent can use to stimulate creativity in her child. Although this list is given for the three–four age group, the activities will suit all three–six-year-olds. They will develop manipulative abilities, stimulate interest in indoor work and promote investigative zeal, develop pride in presentation and provide an outlet for frustration and emotional conflict. It is certainly not an aspect of academic life that should be neglected. (There are more ideas on page 153.)

Drawing activities
1) Chalk on blackboards and slates

2) Wipe down 'magic' slates

3) Using stencils and templates

4) Towards four years your child will begin to use colouring books. Some children take great pride in their skill at colouring within the edges.

5) Graph paper and tracing paper are useful for guiding line.

6) Three-year-olds find great joy in drawing round hands and feet.

7) Copying begins at this age, especially o and x.

8) Your child can draw around wooden blocks and other shapes and create patterns on sugar paper.

Painting
Make sure that the table, floor and your child are protected! You can use various containers for paint pots. Try margarine tubs, ice-cream tubs, tins, plastic egg boxes. At this stage short-handled brushes are best and *large* pieces of paper.

1) Finger painting. Make the paint thick by mixing soap flakes, cold-water starch and cold water in equal amounts.

2) Blow painting using a straw (this can be very messy).

3) Use a candle to draw with, then cover with thin paints. This will create an interesting effect when the paint does not cover the candle wax.

4) Potato prints. Carve shapes into a half-cut potato and dip into paint.

5) Make 'reflections' by folding a rectangular piece of paper in half, then opening it out and printing a shape on one side. Finally fold the sides together again to create the mirror image.

6) Use polystyrene or foam rubber shapes to dip into paint and then make interesting patterns on the paper.

Collages
Here are some creative ideas to make some very colourful and imaginative pictures.

1) Stick shapes on paper. Packets of sticky shapes can be bought and used to produce designs on sugar paper. Three-year-olds are particularly fascinated by this activity. John sat at this creative activity for some time when he would disdain others.

2) Use animal shapes and transport shapes that will complement experience from real life and books. Hannah illustrates her experience in this example:

'What's this?' asked Hannah.

'It's a tiger,' said Mum.

'They got big teeth,' said Hannah. She pasted the shape of a bus over the tiger.

'Why did you do that?' asked Mum.

'Now the bad tiger can't bite me,' said Hannah.

3) Choose from this array of materials for your pictures: Birthday and Christmas cards, magazines, catalogues, straws, seeds, glitter, ribbon, wool, twigs, leaves, feathers, flowers, grass, sweet wrappers, tissue, crepe paper, beads, pasta shapes

Playdough
You can buy playdough but it is very easy and cheap to make.

1 cup plain flour

$\frac{1}{2}$ cup salt

1 cup water

1 tablespoon oil

2 teaspoons cream of tartar

a *little* colour

Mix a little paint or a few drops of food colouring with the water before adding to the rest of the ingredients. Then mix all the ingredients to a paste, pour into a saucepan and cook slowly. Remove when the consistency is right. Cool and knead. Soak the pan quickly. Keep the playdough in an airtight plastic bag in the fridge. (Check regularly for signs of mould.)

Plasticine and playdough are excellent modelling materials, but your child will need you to show her how to roll out spheres and cylinders to 'build' with.

Plastic and wooden block building
There are excellent building sets on the market today. Duplo and Basic Lego, in particular, have sets for the pre-school child.

Collections
It is a good idea now to begin what is a very creative hobby. Encourage your child to collect items such as: badges, postcards, stamps, matchboxes, leaves, flower-pressings, key rings, souvenirs, tickets (bus/train), bottle tops, etc.

SUMMARY

By following the activities in this chapter your child will have established knowledge in her mind that will provide a link between the real world and certain concrete aspects of schooling. This is a wide base of activities and a foundation onto which abstract concepts can gradually be built. By the time your child is four you should have a clear idea of her potential and have discovered latent talent. Tests for this age group are set out on pages 132 and 140.

CHAPTER FIVE

YOUR CHILD FROM FOUR TO FIVE

Your child will very soon be able to build new experience from the activities mentioned in the previous chapter. Concepts will build on already established prerequisite concepts.

At four your child can throw a ball overarm, button up his clothes and some can even lace their shoes. He can draw a circle more accurately and he can also draw a cross with vertical and horizontal arms.

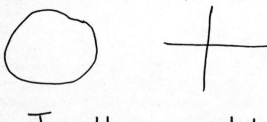

Jonathan, aged 4

He now thinks to himself, 'How do the answers fit to my thoughts?' He 'plays' out loud with grammatical constructions of sentences. He leaves the table spontaneously during learning activities. He is more social now, even more talkative: 'I like this . . .' 'I . . . that . . .'

At four he fabricates and is dogmatic. He is also adventurous, finding he can do 'bad' or naughty things and that there is not total disaster as a result. In art work he is fluid, developing links between related concepts: he draws a cat and then changes it into a man, and finally into a house. By four and a half he can play without using too much incorrect language.

READING

When pre-reading skills have been established in memory, built in through the reading of rhymes, fairy stories and jingles, knowledge of the letters of the alphabet, labelling of familiar objects and pairing words with a picture, reading will begin to progress in earnest.

An integrated 'language' scheme for both speaking and reading works best. It encourages interest through variation and gives practice in reading letters and words. Your child can attempt to read along with you, learn key words, trace letters in sand trays, learn the sounds of those letters, look and say, learn to write short sentences, and to discuss what is being read. How a child learns to read is little understood but experience teaches that input, and output, which create clear mental images, drive that knowledge into memory. The clearest mental image is obtained from real-life experience and from the use of all the senses. Deeper meanings, of words for example, are best remembered because they have more links with other related concepts in long-term memory. There is easier recall, too, because there are close ties with real-life experience to which the 'wires' are open and 'live'.

Besides affording practice, therefore, an integrated language scheme creates extensive links between related concepts, aiding learning and developing creativity. This is the basis to which all future academic knowledge will be bonded. It is indeed the basis for the development of high intelligence.

Picture-Word Pairing

Here is a list of suggested words to pair with a picture:

In the house table, chair, mat, fire, wall, door, window, lamp, curtain, television, vase, flowers, carpet, shelf, kitchen, bedroom, plate, knife, spoon, fork, cup, saucer, bathroom, sink, brush, vacuum cleaner, bed, cupboard, cooker, book, paper, letter, shoe, shirt, jumper, dress, apple, coat, doll, teddy, train, bread, egg, box, bin, pillow, sheet, blanket, banana, soap, tea, coffee, cheese, milk, bacon, telephone

Outside the house garden, path, greenhouse, shed, tree, bush, bird, animal, insect, grass, flower, swing

Parts of the body head, eyes, nose, mouth, ears, chin, neck, shoulder, arm, elbow, wrist, hand, fingers, thumb, chest, tummy (stomach), bottom, leg, foot, toes, knee

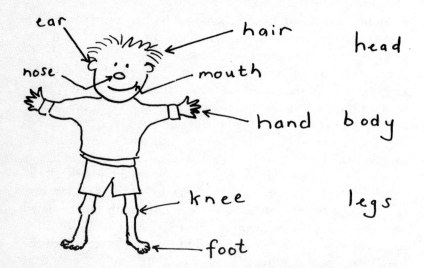

In the street pavement, road (street), lamp-post, post-box, shop, office, pelican crossing, traffic-lights, motorway, car, van, lorry, truck, bicycle, motorbike

People man, woman, lady, girl, boy, policeman, doctor, nurse, dentist, shopkeeper, baby, child (children), teacher, grandad, grandma, uncle, aunt, sister, brother, cousin, friend

Places zoo, sea-side, town, countryside, castle, river, field, museum, shopping centre, supermarket, village

Animals dog, cat, horse, cow, mouse, sheep, lion, elephant, tiger, monkey

Others sky, rain, sun, wind, moon, stars, snow, ice, frost

Abstract jump, run, walk, crawl, slap, tickle, smack, punch, hop, sleep, wake, lie, stand, push, pull, over, under, behind, through, like, hate, kind, cruel, cross (angry), sad, happy

Expressions smile, laugh, cry, shout, speak, talk

Essential words danger, stop, exit, police

It should not be the intention that all these are learnt as reading words, but the meanings should be made clear.

Look and Say

This is best used in conjunction with a Key Words reading scheme (e.g. Ladybird Key Words books). The stilted nature of the text is more than compensated for by the speed at which a child begins to read.

It helps to make a few flash cards, writing one word clearly on each card in lower case lettering (*see* page 49). Show your child four or five cards at a time after you have read a book with him. Don't labour over this, or wait too long for him to attempt the word – your child's distaste of the exercise must be avoided *at all costs*.

Key Words

Third group (*See* page 51 for first and second groups)

about back been before big by call came could did do down first from got go has her here if into just like little look make made me more much must my new no now off old on only or other our out over right see she some their them then there this two up want well went were what when where which who will your

Progress for many children will be fairly slow at first but a few will advance very rapidly. John (at two years of age), within a few weeks, knew at least 100 words from flash cards. It was then time to introduce phonics, reading letter sounds, in order to develop his word-building ability.

Phonics

The first step is to acquaint your child with so-called short vowel sounds and the sounds of the consonants. Letters tied to pictures make the learning more interesting and easier. Programmes like 'Sesame Street' also give life to letters, making them move and speak. A frieze of the phonic alphabet pinned to your child's bedroom wall will stimulate practice, if you refer to it from time to time. The Early Learning Centre and Ladybird Books produce excellent friezes. The Letterland teaching scheme is a novel way of making letters 'live' with pictogram characters representing the sounds of each letter (e.g. Bouncy Ben).

Phonic alphabets can be supplemented by solid letters, through tracing in a sand tray and 'visualising' the letter and sound together. This will give form and depth to the image your child creates in his mind, providing scope to the linkages that can be formed in the memory.

A list of starter books for reading and reading schemes is given at the end of the book (on page 162) along with other learning aids.

WRITING

Your child needs to be competent in the use of a pencil. Tracing over patterns or letters helps as shown in the previous chapter, or simply drawing a picture with a pencil, but ultimately the best practice is freehand copying of shapes and letters.

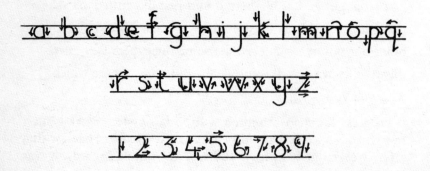

The Phonic Alphabet

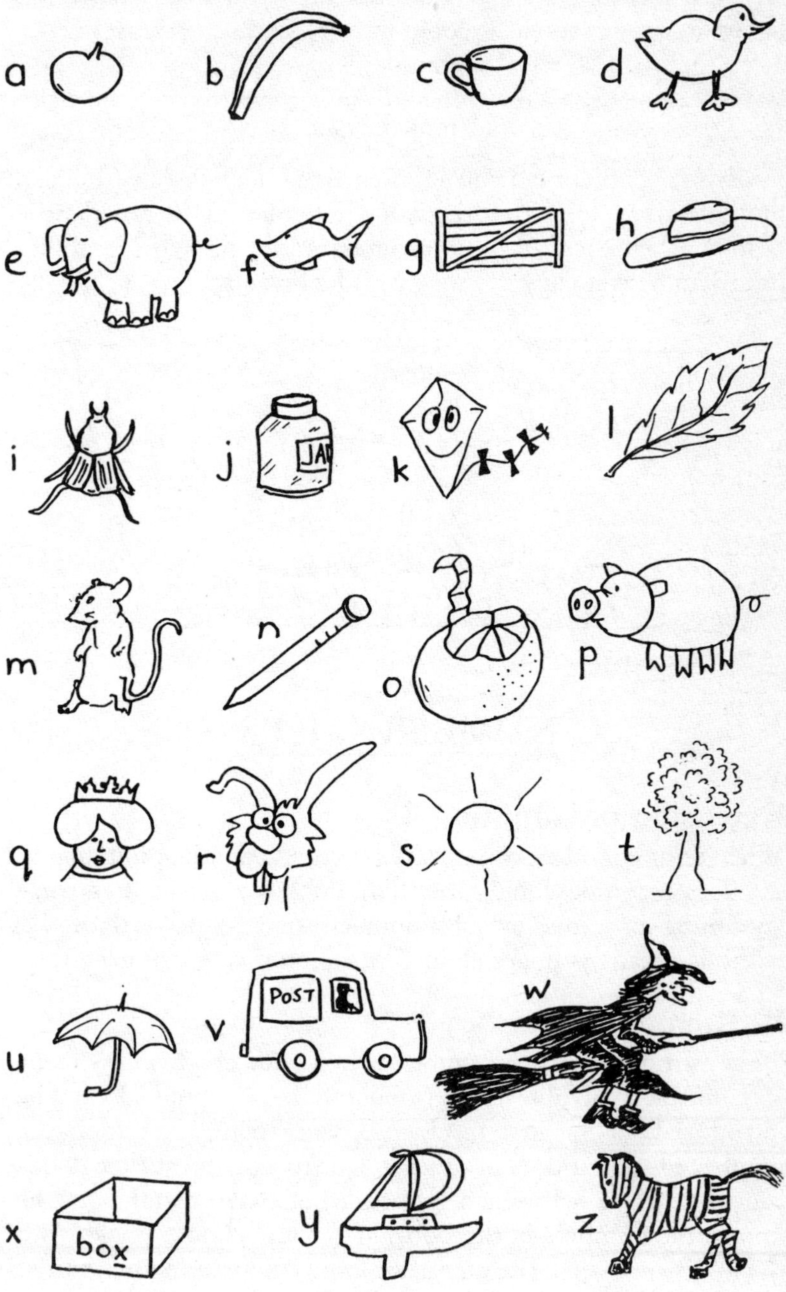
a
b
c
d
e
f
g
h
i
j
JAR
k
l
m
n
o
p
q
r
s
t
u
v
POST
w
x
box
y
z

By now your child should have a wide variety of grammatically correct sentences in his vocabulary. Now that he is speaking well get him to draw a picture and then you write a sentence below it. These sentences could be very simple, such as:

This is a cat.

Here is the car.

Try to get him to tell you a sentence that includes a verb (i.e. a 'doing' word). Some children will want you to write down more than one sentence. As time progresses and his writing ability improves he can copy the sentences he invents:

NUMBER SKILLS

Extension of Counting
When your child can count to ten, extend counting, initially, to 20. This may take longer than you think – there is often some stumbling or omission of numbers such as 13, 16 or 17. Although some younger children can count very competently.

Written Numbers
Only introduce written numbers when your child is *very* facile at counting real objects. Written numbers should always be introduced, in the first instance, linked to the corresponding number of similar dots or objects. Dot-to-dot and sticker books can be used to help teach numbers but make certain that he knows the numbers in the book first. Only choose books with the lower numbers. The pictures can be coloured in afterwards.

1· 2·· 3··· 4···· 5·····
6::: 7:::· 8:::: 9::::· 10:::::

Draughts and Chess are excellent games to form a basis in memory for mathematical concepts that involve special awareness and sense of angle. They also teach a disciplined approach, concentration and train your child in visualising because he has to think several moves ahead.

More Than, Less Than

The terms 'more than' and 'less than' are very little understood by infant children. At this stage pile some wooden bricks on top of each other and say, 'This pile is *more* than this!' (pointing), and then, 'This pile is *less* than this.' After a few sessions pointing this out you can then say, 'Which is more?' and, 'Which is less?'

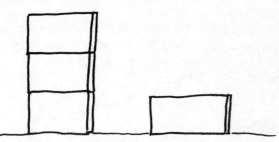

If you extend the meaning of the concept to distance, flat space (area) and quantity (volume), your child will appreciate the full range of meanings of 'more than' and 'less than'.

Adding

When a child first comes to this concept he will be very uncertain unless you explain carefully and demonstrate using concrete examples. Hence:

'I have two sweets and you have three sweets. How many are there altogether?' I ask my young pupil.

'Twotee three,' said Farkhana.

Adding is most clearly shown using wooden cubes from a child's brick set. They should be the same size, volume and colour so that there is no confusion of concepts.

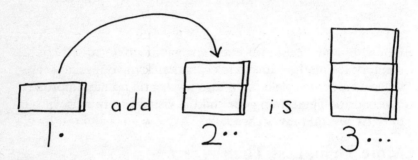

This way of starting to add creates a very clear image in a child's mind because the tower is isolated from background and relates to real life where objects 'grow' upwards from the ground, increasing in height (houses, shops, cars, trees, flowers, etc.). The use of the addition sign is not essential initially.

Shapes

Once again a good set of wooden bricks with a wide variety of shapes is essential to help establish and sort the shapes in your child's memory. Wooden bricks are better than plastic as they are solid and cannot change shape.

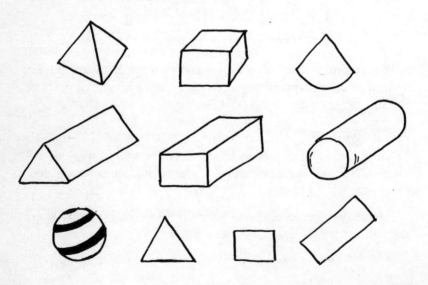

Some names can be introduced now and more when he is sure about those he has learnt. At first try triangle, circle, square, rectangle, cube, and cylinder. (*See also* page 108.)

Telling the time

It is most important when teaching this subject, that a concept like the passing of time and the learning of clock-face times are kept separate. Before introducing the clock to your child make sure that the concept of 'time' is clearly entrenched in memory. Point out to him the passing of the day and relate it to his everyday life at home. You could say, 'Now it is breakfast time. It is morning. Later it will be midday and we will have something more to eat.' At midday say, 'Now it is time for our meal and then it will be afternoon.' In the evening, you can say, 'Soon it will be night-time and we can go to sleep.'

This 'hitching' of the passing of time onto meal times is very effective. The rumbles in a four-year-old's tummy will signal that some time has passed since the last meal.

The Clock

Children can only learn one concept at a time. It is extremely important to teach aspects of time in separate 'packages' as shown. Your child will need much practice before moving on to a new stage. Too many parents attempt to teach a number of aspects at the same time, causing confusion in their child's mind. The rule should be to keep things clear and simple.

Only when the passing of time is fully understood will your children be ready to be introduced to the o'clock times. Point out the position of the long and short hands and relate the time to meal times and bed-time.

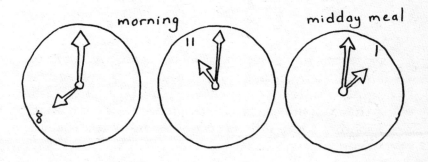

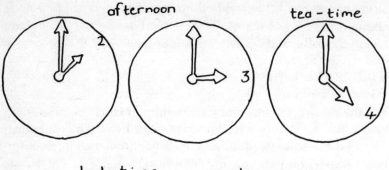

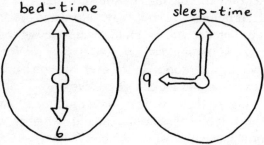

Money

When your child has learnt to count, he can count out 1p coins amounting to the prices of objects (e.g. toys) that you have labelled – choose prices such as 3p, 5p and so on.

Some parents start giving pocket money at this age, but if you do this give only multiples of 1p coins. They also include systems of rewards: 1p for good work, 2p about for excellent work. However, this can be counter-productive when it comes to schoolwork where such a *concrete* reward system is not in operation!

Do not try to teach change at this stage. It will be difficult enough for your child to decipher 3p as three coins by counting. However, children will enjoy using a toy till to put money in and playing a game of shopping with you.

Measurement

Ensure that your child is aware of the concepts of length, weight and capacity. At this stage there is no need to introduce formal units. Only the concepts of length, weight and capacity need to be understood now.

Length Using hand-spans, feet-lengths and a metre stick will ensure that this concept is well understood.

Weight A centre-balance can be used to illustrate the concept of weight. Also balance a small toy on some scales with a piece of plasticine and show your child that the shape of the plasticine does not affect its weight.

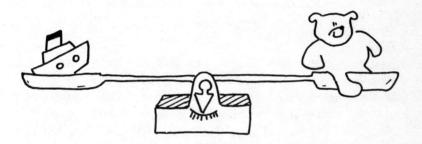

Ask your child, 'Which is heavier, teddy or your toy boat?' Use the words 'same weight' if they are equal.

Volume and capacity After carrying out the investigations in the previous chapter your child should now have a clear understanding of the concept of volume. If he is not sure let him use plastic cups to see how many fill your plastic jug. Say, 'Look! Six cups fill my jug.' This should also link with the concepts of more and less. Show him that the same *volume* of liquid takes different shapes in different containers, and seems to contain less in some than others.

Compass points

Children are able to grasp this concept fairly easily and quickly. Use a magnetic compass to mark the compass points on a large piece of stiff card. Explain that North (N) is over there, and then that South (S) is over there and so on. Next place some sugar paper marked with the compass points on the living-room floor, ask your child to stand in the centre and turn towards the various letters. This gives a sense of rotation and of turning through angles. You can explain that each turn to a new letter is through one right angle.

Symmetry

Some children are able to see symmetry at a very young age, probably because they have inherited an above-average ability to discriminate patterns and have built on this potential through every-day observation of shape and form. Many household objects can be divided into parts of equal size thus having symmetry. Point out to your child where a dividing line separates two identical halves. This can also be illustrated with letters and numbers. In the following examples the door has no symmetry apart from the plane shown because of the handle.

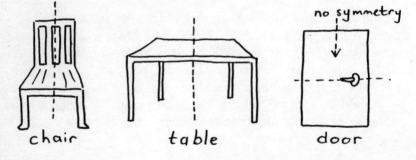

chair   table   door

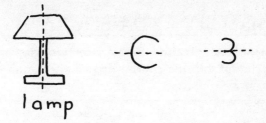

lamp

Butterfly painting Bilateral symmetry is clearly demonstrated using a rectangular piece of drawing paper. Your child needs to fold the paper, open it up, paint on one half and then fold to 'print' the reproduction.

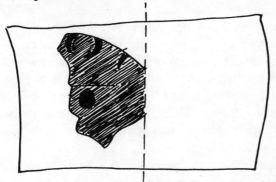

Snowflakes Take a square sheet of coloured or plain paper, fold twice and cut pieces out of the folded edge and the corners. When opened up the paper is in the form of a symmetrical pattern.

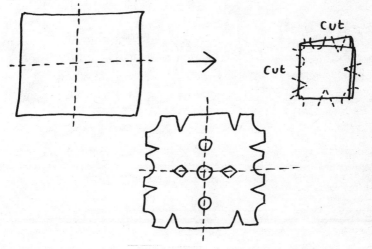

HISTORY AND GEOGRAPHY

A four-year-old has a healthy imagination. One day I took John to the church and into the churchyard where I pointed out the inscription on a gravestone.

'Look! It says 1642. That's a long time ago.'

'Is it as old as Grandma?' he asked.

'Much older. It's older than Grandma's Grandma.'

John's eyes opened with wonder. 'That's *really* old,' he said.

History is best seen and appreciated through real-life experience. Pictures in a book have some meaning but it is difficult to have a realisation of the passing of time. Visiting churches, graveyards, castles and pointing to the year written on old cottages gives a better sense, just as visiting places gives a sense of distance, from home, and height, on top of a hill or mountain. A regular visit to the local museum or an exhibition will also encourage interest. Sometimes historical pageants are staged in castle grounds, but such events do not convey the same sense of history to a small child as they do to an adult.

Many four- to five-year-olds show great interest in some subjects like dinosaurs and this can also convey a sense of history.

SCIENCE AND INVESTIGATIONS

Health and Hygiene

Habits learned at a very early age are likely to stay for the rest of one's life. It might seem like 'nagging' but as long as this does not amount to aversion therapy, a small child will gradually learn. It is fairly easy to explain why certain habits should be followed.

'Brush your teeth and you will grow up looking pretty when you smile.'

'Flies are horrible things. They land on mess and don't wipe it off their feet. Then they go straight away and land on jam and sugar. Don't you think that is very dirty?'

'Sleep is very important. It makes you feel better in the day time.' And, 'If you feel too tired you can't think properly.'

'If you don't eat properly you will get sick.' Or 'Good food keeps you healthy and makes you grow big and strong.'

Statements such as these set up related concepts in memory that others are linked to forming a foundation for life. Although later other considerations may over-rule, such advice will always be remembered.

Places to Visit (*See also* pages 172–183)

Much science can be learnt on visits. The zoo is an excellent place for a child to learn. Many word meanings can be learnt in one day on such an outing. Here is a list of possible examples:

big bigger biggest tall taller tallest fat skinny long wiggley poison hairy striped spotted claws trunk hump fierce roar hiss crush run jump hop crawl paw pant stalk howl snarl copy whistle climb lion tiger elephant crocodile monkey wolf parrot eagle bear insects camel giraffe penguin sea-lion shark

bear

sea-lion

kangaroo

leopard

At the sea-side

There is a great deal of science to be learned both on the beach and nearby – at the fair, for example. Here are some more word meanings to learn:

sea waves deep shallow sandy green blue salty sand soft hard pebbles crabs shells rocks seaweed jelly-fish swings roundabout Big Wheel slides boats ships swim sail

Fruit and Vegetables

Explain to your child that these contain seeds which grow into new plants. Show him the seeds inside an apple or an orange. Other fruits and vegetables to examine and to talk about generally are bananas, blackberries, blackcurrants, cherries, tomatoes, peas, nuts, pears, mushrooms, cabbages, onions, carrots.

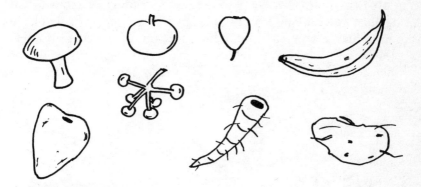

In the Park or Countryside

Let your child collect leaves, wind-blown seeds such as ash, conkers, pine cones, grasses like bulrushes, berries, bulbs and fungi (toadstools and mushrooms). Let your child blow off dandelion seeds to 'find out' what time it is (the number of blows represents the hour), and put a buttercup up to his neck to see if he 'likes butter' – if he does there will be a yellow glow. Talk about colours, shapes and a little about the purposes of leaves, flowers and seeds. Show him a few of the poisonous plants such as deadly nightshade, some toadstools, yew berries, etc. Point out birds that you can recognise on a country walk. The names are not that important, more what the birds are doing. 'Look, that bird is fishing in the lake. It has got a long beak and stands very still.'

On the riverside there are further topics to discuss including fish, fishing, river water, pollution, river animals, and so on.

In the Garden

Your child can continue his investigations by asking you about earthworms, insects, small animal life, trees, bushes, flowers and grasses. Make him aware that some insects such as wasps, bees, certain beetles and spiders should not be touched as they can bite or sting.

Pets

If your child has a pet, it is an ideal opportunity to explain about caring, growth and development, and even birth. You can, therefore, involve your child in feeding, cleaning, and simply watching how animals behave. Caring for pets will have an influence on your child in later life, for, as the poet says, 'He loveth best who loveth best all things both great and small, for the dear God who loveth us, He made and loveth all' (with apologies to Coleridge).

Sound

Your child will find it fascinating to listen to a sea-shell. The echoes inside the shell sound like waves breaking on the sea-shore. Stringed and percussion instruments create sound by vibrations and he can try playing or listening to a guitar or tambourine. There are many other examples to investigate.

Weather

These are many topics to discuss about climate, the seasons and the weather. Here are a few; rainbow colours, rain, snow, sleet, ice, hail, wind, thunderstorms, sun, cloud types, temperature, thermometer, barometer.

Forces

These can be investigated simply by watching 'stopping' and 'starting'. And also by looking at athletes and different sports either on television or in real life.

MUSIC

Many activities for three-year-olds are also suitable for four-year-olds. It is worth remembering that music played in a house is a fairly constant input. What is 'put in' generally remains for life. If range and form are limited and do not link with deep emotion, there may also be limited related concepts in memory associated with music.

Although music with a strong beat may elicit a desire to dance in your young child, he also needs experience of good tunes and more complex music. Later in life such knowledge in memory can be built upon: there is no danger in introducing young children to the 'finer things of life', as long as it does not become drudgery. Linking music to dance and ballet, to stories and films will develop a wealth of worthwhile associations. For instance, one could explain the story behind a piece of music like *Má Vlast* or ask him to make up a story to Holst's 'Mars' from *The Planets* or simply watch Walt Disney's film *Fantasia*. These are just a few suggestions to give you some ideas.

ART AND CREATIVE ACTIVITIES

Children now have rapidly developing manipulative abilities and will graduate towards producing more detailed work, being more adept in the use of a pencil and using thin crayons for colouring in pictures. One of the aims at this stage should be to develop a greater awareness of shape (in real life and through handling and playing with bricks, and using stencils, etc.) and patterns. The latter, in particular, will provide prerequisite skill for the learning of abstract symbols like letters and numbers. By extending the creative activities listed in the previous chapter and including more ideas from Chapter 6 your child will be able to develop new knowledge through the use of the senses and provide avenues for considerable creative links in his mind.

SUMMARY

At this stage of a child's development, it is not so much the names of things that are important, but the development of bodies of knowledge in memory that illustrate scientific principles. It is enough to know that white light consists of several colours and that is why we see a multi-coloured light in the sky before we even know its name is a rainbow. Although specifics are useful to illustrate general truths, the aim should be to make clear the general, then work down towards specifics. For example, if one had never seen a tree before it would be rather pointless to show a child a tree for the first time and say:

'This is an oak.'

There would be a tendency to ask 'What is it for?'

Children learn best by learning general characteristics of a concept (e.g. by looking at a wide variety of trees), and *then* picking out specifics. It is important to know what a tree *is* in general before talking about pine trees, ash trees, weeping willows and so on. So it is better to say from the beginning, 'This is a tree, and that over there is a tree'. Thus he can see for himself the general characteristics of the concept (tall, trunk, branches, leaves, static, growing, producing, seeds, etc.).

Tests for this age group are set out at the end of the book (*see* pages 132 and 142).

CHAPTER SIX

YOUR CHILD AT FIVE PLUS

At five a child is capable of doing most of the essential, physical activities required of her. She can brush her own teeth, comb her hair and wash her face. She is adept at using a knife and fork, and by six can use the telephone fairly well (although this depends on knowledge of written numbers). She can skip well and balance on one foot for several seconds.

She draws a recognisable man:

Adrian, aged 5½

A child aged between five and six can also draw many patterns well. (Although some children develop this ability at younger ages). For example:

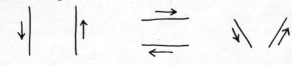

The inability to draw certain lines until they are several years old does not mean that children do not recognise oblique, horizontal and vertical patterns. Real-life practice with solid objects, including even the ground beneath their feet, will have developed this. There certainly is a step up to recognising the vertical *edge* of a wall as a vertical line, but this is not a considerable jump. A lamp-post is seen as a thick line, fences are made up of several 'lines' and the transition from real-life to two-dimensional strokes is relatively easy for a child to achieve. At this stage it is manipulative practice that your child is lacking, and it is that specific practice that establishes a link between recognising line and reproducing it. Similar patterns seem to be stored together in memory where possible and this makes recall easier. A search for 'cat' will immediately recall 'mat', 'sat', 'hat', 'bat', etc. in an older child who can quickly distinguish the initial or first letter shapes. Younger children, however, do not always have either sufficient knowledge in memory to do this easily or sufficient practice in the discernment of different shaped letters. The practice, itself, will develop as a related concept which will exert a measure of control over discernment. It does this through linkages between the shapes of letters. This is the age at which the forging of links between real-life experience and abstract symbols and patterns is so important. Success in early school life depends on such links. At this age most children in the U.K. start primary school.

Between five and six your child is able to keep time to music and has a better sense of time duration, although how precise that sense of time is will depend on what she has learnt. This sense of the passing of time will also lead to your child being able to construct or imitate simple story plots. There will be more meaningful questions from her although the depth of meaning will depend on the quality of experience from the previous two years. She will be protective towards younger siblings and can also be obedient and dependable.

A Launching Pad

By now two fundamental developments should have occurred:

a) There should be extensive development of real-life related concepts within memory. These concepts should reflect every fundamental aspect of schoolwork from sorting groups of similar objects to a wide knowledge of word meanings.

b) Within this development there needs to be appreciation of form and pattern so that the abstract experiences of school-work can easily link into memory.

If these developments are lacking in any major respects it may lead to failure at the outset and consequent loss of confidence by your child. If this is put succinctly and taken to the extreme, it means, as I have stated before, that a child who plays outside each and every day on her cycle up to five years of age, learns colloquialisms from other children and is never talked to by her parents, except for disciplinary purposes, will have a limited number of related concepts in her memory. In addition, there will be little depth to established meanings. Such a child will have only a superficial understanding of the world (although practice may ensure that she is verbally quick and good in a manipulative and physical sense). She is, therefore, very unlikely to succeed in a school environment and even if the potential is there it may not be realised unless the child has a high level of motivation.

ENGLISH

Spelling

As a child learns to read and write she will need the skills that accompany good writing. One of the skills that needs to be developed is spelling. Although reading may help a child's ability to write what she means, that is to express herself, it is, essentially, like listening, a skimming exercise. When we read we learn about story form, glean ideas and find out about people and their emotions but we do not learn where to put every full stop or examine each word for spelling. Skills such as these are best learnt separately and words are best remembered when grouped according to similar sounds and letter combinations.

When your child has learnt phonics and, say, five groups of two- or three-letter words with similar shapes, you can use these to form the basis for the beginning of short spelling tests. Each group should include only one vowel sound. These short vowel words are divided into the following groups:

Group 1

at	man	bat	bad	bag	cam	bap
an	can	cat	cad	fag	jam	cap
	ban	fat	dad	gag	ham	gap
	fan	hat	fad	lag	ram	lap
	pan	mat	had	rag	sam	map
	ran	pat	lad	tag		nap
	tan	rat	mad	wag		rap
		sat	sad	nag		tap

Group 2

off	not	pod	bog	cop
on	cot	cod	hog	mop
of	hot		dog	lop
	pot		log	top
	dot			hop
	rot			
	tot			

Group 3

men	bet	bed	beg	hem
den	met	led	leg	
pen	pet			
ten	set			
	vet			
	let			
	jet			

Group 4

in	bin	bit	bid	big	him	hip
it	din	fit	did	dig	rim	pip
	tin	hit	hid	fig	dim	lip
	fin	kit	kid	pig		sip
	gin	lit	lid	wig		tip
	pin	pit		gig		rip
	sin	sit				nip
	tin					
	win					

Group 5

up	bun	but	bud	bug	gum	cup
	fun	cut	dud	dug	hum	pup
	gun	gut	mud	rug	mum	sup
	nun	hut		hug	rum	
	pun	nut		mug	tum	
	run	rut		tug	sum	
	sun					

An additional stimulus to learning spellings can be provided by asking your child to unjumble words:

ocw   c _____ eats grass and gives milk

By giving your child such an activity you force her to create the mental image of the word in order to match with something in memory. This establishes a clear link between the sound of the word and the shape of it.

Reading

Once your child can recognize many words in text and can sound out letters, you will need to consolidate her progress by spelling words out phonically, emphasising single letter sounds and double blends.

Some words, however, cannot be read in this way and she will only learn them by repetition in the general course of reading, by writing them down on a piece of paper with an accompanying picture where possible, or by having oddities in word structure pointed out to her (e.g. lamb with its silent 'b').

Writing

Your child should be able to speak a large number of grammatically correct sentences by now. She should also be fairly competent at writing the letters and setting down some sentences. It is not too big a step now to ask her to write a slightly longer piece; this should be one that comes from a real-life activity that has aroused her interest, or a story recently seen in a film or on television that has captured her imagination. The *live* pictures imprinted on memory are most easily translated into living words. She can recall the images and hold them in mental view while she writes down what she 'sees'. The best results often occur after watching Disney cartoons or after visits to interesting places, such as the zoo or fairground. You can suggest to your child that she draws a picture at the end of a piece of writing and 'signs' her name.

Handwriting When your child can write well on her own, you can start introducing a few 'rules' by showing her how to write on lined paper. Draw wide lines on blank paper, write sentences down carefully so that she can copy, emphasise the capitals at the beginning of each sentence and make the full stop very definite:

Point out that letters like **p**, **g** and **y** 'sit' on the line. Many children are confused by **b** and **d**, and **n** and **h**. Others write letters and numbers back to front:

+' for 4   S for 2

MATHEMATICS

By this age many children should have a relatively sophisticated group of 'basic' concepts like counting, addition, subtraction, measurement and shape. They should also be able to link these concepts with abstract symbols – number symbols (1,2,3,4 etc), + (plus), and – (minus) – and have an appreciation of units of length and weight in particular.

Shapes

The names of all shapes can be learnt now.

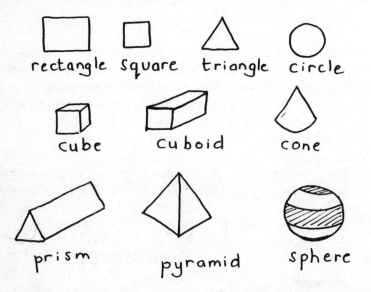

rectangle   square   triangle   circle

cube   cuboid   cone

prism   pyramid   sphere

When teaching your child about shapes relate them to real life by pointing out similar shapes in her environment. Involve your child with one shape at a time until you feel she knows it well, then revise from time to time when learning the other shapes. Such a system of constant revision effects firm establishment in long-term memory, thus ensuring that the 'wires' to that concept are opened and 'live'. The link to real-life knowledge is extremely important: when your child looks at a brick she will 'see' not only size, weight, colour and texture but also an oblong or rectangle and a cuboid, together with the associated words – straight, sharp, corner, cuboid, rectangle, brown, etc. As her senses extend her world, the links between related concepts will be in constant use, ensuring easier recall of information when it is needed. This is how practice can be most effective, contributing to *overlearning* and achieving a form of *saturation* of one small area of memory. The ever-open links to real life then ensure that the information is not lost in its original form. For example, recently I returned to a house I once lived in. The routes and patterns about the house were similar to what I had recalled but the house, itself, had begun to approximate to the general picture of any house and it was only oddities that had remained in my mind and were correct. Thus some of the information about the home had been lost.

Building on Knowledge

These 'general pictures' of concepts established in memory are vitally important in learning. In memory we have, for example, the general idea of 'a street'. When we encounter a new street we match the 'general' images so that we know that this is 'a street', and link with other concepts like length and width (of street), pavement, lamp-post and the oddities that make that street unique.

We learn best by the gradual modification of what is in memory. The lines and patterns that a baby discerns can gradually be built up into recognition of shapes, both two- and three-dimensional, and eventually of many real-life objects.

The fact that a new-born baby must have something in memory to interpret the environment (though this may be only a rudimentary perception of pattern) indicates that not everything we know is learnt. Without *something* in memory to match with the environment we could not attribute meaning. The concept of building on what is similar in memory is a very important one. Indiscriminate learning as a preparation for schoolwork will result in wide variations in ability to succeed in school, regardless of potential. A sensible approach for a parent tutor is to prepare 'learning plans' where knowledge is built up in stages so that little modification is necessary to develop an understanding of new concepts.

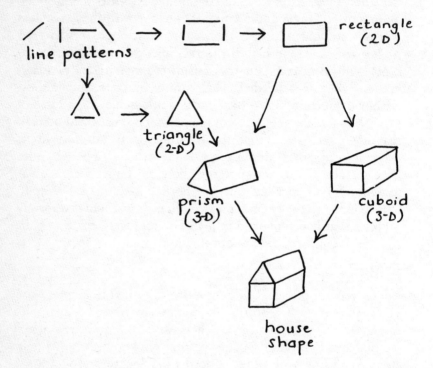

Subtraction (Taking Away)

One of the first ideas that becomes entrenched in a child's mind is the one that says, 'That thing has gone. Now there is nothing left.'

'Where has Daddy's car gone, Mummy?'

'He's taken it to work.'

The final picture she may have had before she went to bed was of a driveway and Daddy's car on it. In the morning, the superimposed image of the driveway in her mind shows the 'gap' that represents her Daddy's car. This is *zero*. So,

$$1 - 1 = 0$$

The idea of 'everything's gone' should be represented by a very definite concept in memory. As a mental image it could be expressed as:

However, 3 − 1 = 2 represents an entirely new concept. Something is removed but there is something remaining. A child has to create a new link in order to establish meaning to this fresh experience.

Furthermore, the clarity of the image you create is all important in creating the necessary link:

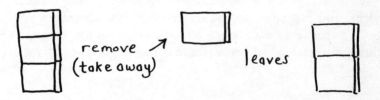

remove ↗
(take away)   leaves

The first step in the learning process is to establish the connection between a vertical pile of three bricks (image 1), removing one brick (image 2), and leaving two bricks (image 3). For the concept to become established each step must be clearly indicated to your child. Explain what you are doing as you do it, leaving time for a clear mental picture to be created in her mind each time:

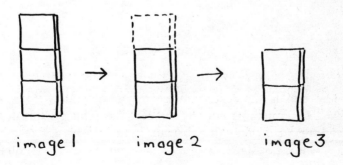

image 1   image 2   image 3

Your child should repeat the activity and the words:

'Here are three bricks.'

'I take one away.'

'Two are left.'

Practice like this using different numbers (up to five only) will establish the concept in memory. The activity could then be repeated using a take-away (minus) sign as well as saying the words 'take away'. Eventually, the whole operation can be reduced to abstract symbols. However, with about five minutes a day being spent on subtraction, the total learning time from beginning to overlearning will be several weeks.

The above represents an ideal learning situation: the illustration of a concept or item of information using concrete (real-life) objects, clear presentation of elements of the concept or item, and a gradual introduction of related abstract symbols, with practice at each stage so that *saturation* is ensured and links are established between the concrete and the abstract.

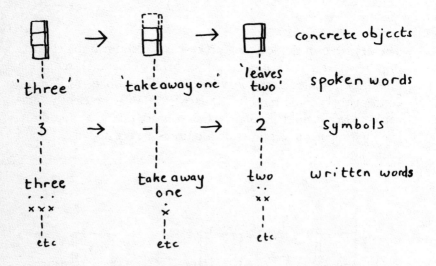

The aim is that every abstract symbol and word is firmly linked to something concrete in real life. This creates depth of meaning: in a sense the abstract is no longer abstract at this level as it is not free from concrete or representational qualities.

Addition

In a similar manner to the step-by-step introduction of the −
(minus) symbol, the + (plus) symbol can be introduced to
addition sums. However, many children become confused when
asked to complete a mix of addition and subtraction. This is
because these concepts are not firmly established in linkages to
the symbols.

Money and Shopping

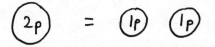

An initial difficulty is the establishing of one object (2p) as
representing two objects (1p and 1p). Although this concept is
clearly illustrated when a brick of size 2 is placed alongside two
bricks of size 1:

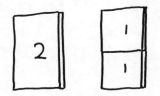

Money presents new problems because some coins of high
denomination are smaller than those of low denomination. In
order to overcome this problem point to the 2p coin, tap twice
on it and say, 'This says two pence.'

Let her count rows of 2p and 1p coins, tapping twice on each
2p coin as she gets to it:

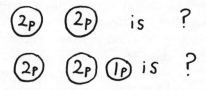

Shopping activities can be extended when she is certain of
taking away. You can be the shopkeeper and she the customer,
and in that way you show her how to work out change. One
day that magic moment will come when you say: 'Would you
like to be the shopkeeper?'

You will need to spend much time using low denomination coins before advancing to the next step with the higher denomination coins. The establishment of a concept and its links to other related concepts is more important than racing onto using bigger numbers.

Sharing

The teaching of the concept of sharing is not too difficult to integrate into your child's normal pattern of life. It can be started at this age, or even much younger, by emphasising fairness and the need to be equal in distribution. You may buy a toy for one child, and then buy the equivalent for her sister or brother. Sharing equally should be established as a concept in memory long before beginning division:

equal shares of a cake

equal shares of sweets

The word 'half' can be used at this stage (although many five-years-olds are very clear about this concept already), and even 'quarter'. It is, however, best not to labour over symbols.

When your child is clear about numbers it provides good grounding to get her to share sweets, 1p coins and other objects between one, two or even three people. Numbers, however, should be kept very low, and there should be no remainders. As always the learning of the concept takes precedence over sheer manipulation of numbers. Again, symbols need not be introduced (e.g. ÷ or ⌐) unless your child is exceptionally quick, and even then it should be done in clear stages.

Tables

The learning of tables is very useful for life, for easing the learning of division and for the cancelling of fractions and other maths activities later in school life. However, the rote learning of tables represents superficial meaning in memory, and without relating this pure skill to real life, certain mathematical concepts will not be understood in future schoolwork. It will not be necessary, however, to relate every skill to real-life experience whenever it is used. When multiplying number symbols (like 2, 3, 4 etc.) in a sum there is not always a clear mental picture of deeper meaning in the mind but there should be an associated 'fleeting' mental image which indicates that understanding (deep meaning) is there.

Multiplication as a concept is closely tied to addition as a concept. The two can be tied together by using toy men:

Two legs... Two legs... Two legs...

Ask your child, 'How many men are there?' and 'How many legs have they?'

This activity can be extended using buttons, sweets or wooden cubes:

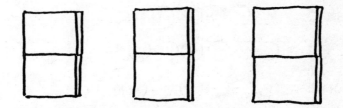

This latter activity makes the concept particularly clear, because your child does not have to extract that concept from many others. For instance in the toy men illustrated above concepts such as 'arms', 'legs', 'heads', 'hats', 'men', 'toys' are all linked closely together.

The idea of several sets of two in the Two Times Table must be clearly recognised before introducing any new symbols.

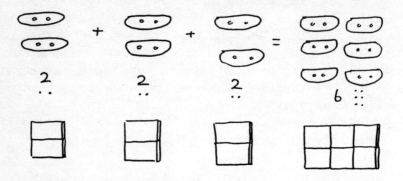

Eventually, after much practice the abstract form of multiplication can be tied to addition:

$3 \times 2 = $ (· ·) (· ·) (· ·) $=$ (· · · · · ·) 6

The Two Times Table

$1 \times 2 = $ (· ·)   2

$2 \times 2 = $ (· ·)(· ·)   4

$3 \times 2 = $ (· ·)(· ·)(· ·)   6

$4 \times 2 = $ (· ·)(· ·)(· ·)(· ·)   8

$5 \times 2 = $ (· ·)(· ·)(· ·)(· ·)(· ·)   10

$6 \times 2 = $ (· ·)(· ·)(· ·)(· ·)(· ·)(· ·)   12

$7 \times 2 = $ (· ·)(· ·)(· ·)(· ·)(· ·)(· ·)(· ·)   14

$8 \times 2 = $ (· ·)(· ·)(· ·)(· ·)(· ·)(· ·)(· ·)(· ·)   16

$9 \times 2 = $ (· ·)(· ·)(· ·)(· ·)(· ·)(· ·)(· ·)(· ·)(· ·)   18

$10 \times 2 = $ (· ·)(· ·)(· ·)(· ·)(· ·)(· ·)(· ·)(· ·)(· ·)(· ·)   20

Later, the Five Times Table and then the Ten Times Table can be developed in a similar manner.

Telling The Time

When your child is clear about the o'clock times, move on to half-past the hours but still working slowly and steadily on one stage at a time.

morning: breakfast time

lunch time

tea-time

bed-time

Finally, introduce quarter-past and quarter-to. Until she knows the Five Times Table, minutes past and minutes to are going to be difficult for her. As I have already mentioned, this should be done in carefully presented stages or concepts will become confused in the child's mind.

Measurement

Length By now, your child will be able to count the centimetres on a ruler. Get her to measure the lengths of various objects: a book, pencil, spoon, table mat, or small toys. She can measure longer lengths with a tape-measure, depending on her ability to count, of course.

Weight It is very difficult for your child, without the knowledge of 1,000, to see real meaning in weights such as 500g, 250g and so on. A few children, however, are aware of large numbers and it will be possible to point out that an item of food weighs ½kg, ¼kg and so on.

However, a new concept is being introduced here, that of two halves equalling one whole, or four quarter kilogram weights equalling 1 kilogram (kg). Using a balance this is easy to illustrate (two ½kg weights balance 1kg, four ¼kg weights balance 1kg). It is not normally the time to link these fractions with 250g and 500g, although some pre-school children learn the association fairly quickly if they are involved with helping mother cook.

Simple fractions can be illustrated by cutting an apple or orange in half, and then into quarters.

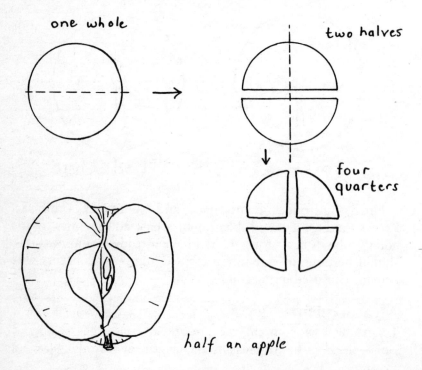

one whole   two halves

four quarters

half an apple

The calculator and computer can be used to show counting up to large numbers but in reality weight and volume are little understood until well into secondary school. The fundamental problem is that there are not related concepts for large numbers in memory. For a child to appreciate 500, for example, she would need to practise counting piles of various objects to 500 and then to have the abstract symbol introduced gradually. This is, obviously, very time consuming and, therefore, the true *meaning* of large numbers becomes a 'gap' in knowledge, even when your child is doing addition sums with thousands, hundreds, tens and units, because these are done mechanically.

Arrays can solve some of the problems. An array is a number pattern and a 100 array, as shown below, will for example, show that 50 is half-way between 0 and 100, and that 25 is a quarter of 100. The use of arrays will supplement your child's learning that 500g is the weight of a packet of sugar. However, for a 1,000 array a knowledge of at least the Ten Times Table is essential because space considerations dictate that a 1,000 array must be set out in sets of tens, not ones. Arrays can, of course, help with general mathematical problems too.

A One Hundred Array

1	2	3	4	5	6	7	8	9	10
11	12	13	14	15	16	17	18	19	20
21	22	23	24	25	26	27	28	29	30
31	32	33	34	35	36	37	38	39	40
41	42	43	44	45	46	47	48	49	50
51	52	53	54	55	56	57	58	59	60
61	62	63	64	65	66	67	68	69	70
71	72	73	74	75	76	77	78	79	80
81	82	83	84	85	86	87	88	89	90
91	92	93	94	95	96	97	98	99	100

Volume Similar problems apply to volume. You can point out to your child whole litres of drinks in cartons and petrol when Dad is filling up his tank at the garage. However, unless your child is fully aware of the *deep* meaning of large numbers, future related knowledge (e.g. $1/10$ of a kilogram or 0.1 of a litre) will be difficult to teach properly.

Using the calculator and computer
Children love playing with calculators so you will have no trouble getting your child to use the calculator to *check* the answers to her sums. She can also investigate large numbers:

$$10 + 10 + 10 + 10 \ldots \ldots$$
$$20 + 20 + 20 + 20 \ldots \ldots$$

This is very important because it gives her the 'sense' of how much bigger, say, 600 is than ten or 20, an important prerequisite to a knowledge of place value (hundreds, tens, units, decimal places, etc.). Working out sums on a calculator also establishes a clearly defined link between symbols and the concepts of addition, subtraction, multiplication and division.

A much wider usefulness can be attributed to the computer for, in addition to pure games like Nintendo, there are excellent software programmes on tape and disk, some of which are detailed later in the book. However, apart from educational software, it is important that your child uses both a computer and calculator at as early a stage as possible so that she is familiar with basic processes and the limitations of both. When she starts school she will be confident when using such technology and also display an intelligent awareness of the purpose of the calculator and computer.

Computer learning programmes are undoubtedly useful aids to learning but the hands-on use of concrete material and the learning of abstract symbols by using all the senses provides superior learning. Furthermore, working closely with a parent with such materials provides a close bond that results in strong motivation and the link between learning and emotional factors is long-lasting. Although both a calculator and computer have a place in schoolwork (for practice and consolidation work), as a teaching aid they can never replace the encouragement and individual attention of a parent.

Word Meanings In Mathematics

Many of the difficulties children encounter at school are not with Maths at all but rather with word and symbol meanings. Confusion can occur, in particular, where two or three words seem to apply to the same activity but represent different concepts. For example, a child may know how to take away but be unable to find the difference, or how many 'less than'. This is because taking away is a clearly defined removal of an object:

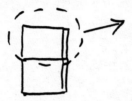

'Difference' is a comparison activity which requires counting on:

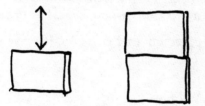

The term 'less than' often requires counting back on a *number line*:

2 less than 5 is 3

Number Line

$$\begin{array}{c} 5 \\ 4 \\ 3 \\ 2 \\ 1 \\ 0 \end{array}$$

Other word meanings and symbols that may cause confusion are: more, more than, count on, count back, different ways of writing sums, placeholder, subtraction, addition, equals =, less than <, greater than >

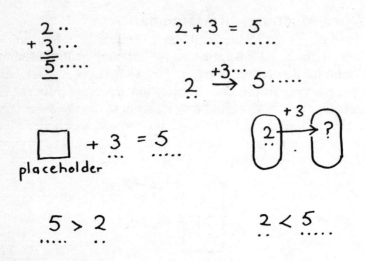

Problem Solving

Essentially, problem solving will involve worded examples which embrace more than one concept. For example:

One toy costs 5p and another costs 3p. If I give the shopkeeper 10p, how much change do I get?

Concept 1   Addition

$$
\begin{array}{r}
5p \\
+\,3p \\
\hline
8p \\
\hline
\end{array}
$$

Concept 2   Subtraction

$$
\begin{array}{r}
10p \\
-\,8p \\
\hline
2p \\
\hline
\end{array}
$$

The above problem is more complicated than simply separating two concepts because there is an inference that you must

find out how much the two toys cost together and your child
must know that 'change' refers to what is left over from the cost
of the toys.

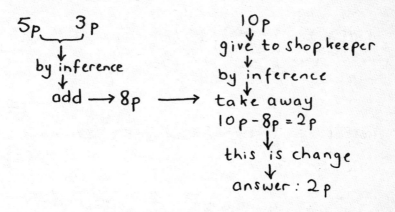

It is clear from even this simple example that to effectively
solve problems your child needs practice not only in sums but in
word meanings. She will also need practice in analysing the
units or elements of the problem that need to be solved at each
stage.

Stage 1 → skim for word meanings → Stage 2
                                          ↓
                                    dissect out
                        piece   the units of
Stage 4 ← together ← Stage 3 ←   the problem
        these units
        and add symbols
   ↓
Solve
the
Sums   → ANSWER

Another problem which illustrates the technique of analysis
and laying out each stage clearly in pictures to link with
memory is illustrated in the following example:

Jane is half as old as John. If John is 14, how old is Jane?

My pupil, Farkhana, does not understand the meaning of 'half'. So together, we reduce the problem to sharing sweets between two people:

half of two   [muffin] | [muffin]   is 1   [muffin]

half of six   (oo) (oo) (oo) | (oo)(oo)(oo) is 3

half of fourteen   is 7

It is now a short jump to 'sharing' years between Jane and John.

INVESTIGATIONS

You can expand your child's exploration of his world by extending visits to markets, castles, fairs, the sea-side, country houses, zoos, museums, children's workshops, farms, organised visits to fire stations, police stations, boat trips, factory trips and many others. Try to let her have a souvenir of as many trips as possible so that you can talk about these visits again.

There are many other activities that can be introduced to develop a wide range of interests and abilities. These could include: making a picture, playing with balloons, building Lego sets and Meccano, playing war games, pressing flowers, examining insects, investigating magnets, cooking, experimenting with the displacement of water (in the bath or sink), playing dice games (Ludo, Snakes and Ladders), darts, Chess, card games, exploring topics such as space, rockets and satellites, discussing size etc. with the help of a book like the *Guinness Book of Records*.

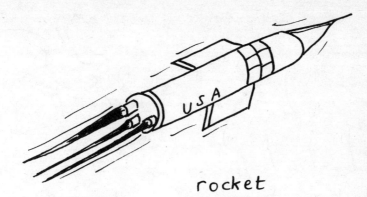

rocket

You can stimulate your child's interest by playing guessing games using drawings you have made, or pictures you have cut out. Here are some examples of such 'puzzles':

I am long
What am I ?

I am small
What am I ?

I am fierce
What am I ?

I am big
What am I?

I run away
What am I?

MUSIC

It is important that you as a parent build up in your child a wide base of interest in listening patterns. What you introduce her to at this age and express an interest in will remain for the rest of her life. It is not enough to inculcate a sense of rhythm through pop music. You will need to introduce her to a wide variety of tunes and subtleties of harmony by letting her listen to film music and songs, show music, country and western, children's songs and classical music. There is no need to make listening a sit-down and learn time. The beauty of listening to music is that it can be an accompaniment to other activities. As far as choice of music is concerned, a famous conductor of classical music had a rule to guide him in assessing good music: if there was not a good tune he would say it was not good music. This is good advice when choosing music for children too. Examples of much-liked classical music include:

Dvořák – *The New World Symphony*
Elgar – *Enigma Variations*
Handel – *Messiah*
Holst – *The Planets* (suite)
Mendelssohn – *Symphony No. 3* Overture: *The Hebrides* (Fingal's Cave)
Mussorgsky – *Night on the Bare Mountain*
Ravel – *Boléro*

Rimsky-Korsakov – *Tsar Sultan: Flight of the bumble bee*
Tchaikovsky – *The Nutcracker: Dance of the Sugar Plum Fairy*
   and *The Sleeping Beauty*
Wagner – *Die Walküre: Ride of the Valkyries*

ART AND CREATIVE ACTIVITIES

At this age your child has greater manipulative abilities and the creative activities she can be included in are many. Here are just a few suggestions.

Drawing Your child's skill could be extended to copying and tracing as well as free drawing, using different pencils, charcoal and crayons.

Painting There is a wide range of activities available using different brushes. Your child can now use an easel as well as painting at a table. She can 'splash' paint, using a lolly stick or an old toothbrush to spread it. An old plant spray container, washed out, can be used. Toy shops like the Early Learning Centre sell palettes and box paints, and a wide variety of such paints can be used, e.g. from water-paints to acrylic.

Your child can also paint with sponges, real-life objects like hands, feet, leaves, vegetables and fruit, and there are rollers you can use for roller painting. She can also blow paint through straws and put substances in the paint to create various textures: soap in the paint can create pictures through the blowing of bubbles (bubble paints).

Paper Try sugar paper, cartridge paper, card, newspaper, wax papers, satin paper.

Folding Paper folded in half on painted shapes demonstrates symmetrical patterns.

Modelling Materials for use include plaster of Paris, playdough, clay (some forms do not need firing) with pipe cleaners, plasticine, chicken wire with papier mâché and other materials from toy shops. Junk modelling can be fun using cardboard boxes, egg boxes, cartons and other materials readily available at home.

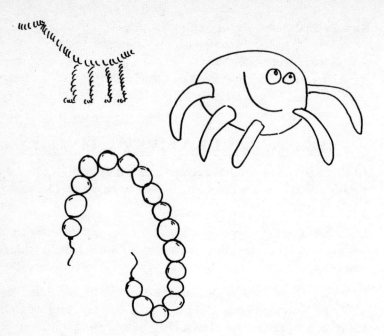

Glues These include P.V.A., Gloy, paper glue, spirit glue (stronger).

Collages These can be made with fabric, sand, sequins, beads, feathers, seeds, leaves, shells, stones, sawdust, wood shavings, egg shells, coloured paper, sticks, etc. The whole effect can be varnished when it is finished.

Sewing, knitting Young children find these activities difficult. Sewing cards and the use of a bobbin for French knitting can be used.

Rafia This can be used for basketwork and model making.

Woodwork Sets of tools can be bought and used with off-cuts of soft wood for hammering and nailing (a vice is required for sawing). These activities should, of course, be done under adult supervision.

Baking This can be creative in shaping and making patterns on biscuits etc. or icing cakes.

There are more ideas listed at the end of the book (*see* page 153).

SUMMARY

The year before school is probably the most important time in a child's academic life. Experience gained just prior to entering school will determine whether your child fits easily into the academic environment or finds this extremely difficult to do. If she is well prepared she will have in memory a wide understanding of concepts in all school disciplines and be well acquainted with certain abstract symbols in language and Mathematics (i.e. letters and numbers). The very fact that your child has been led with some purpose in learning at home, will ensure that she does not find entry to school an introduction to a totally alien environment. Pleasurable associations with learning with a parent will readily transfer to the classroom situation, as long as some element of home education is continued so that any outstanding difficulties encountered at school are ironed out. Tests for this age group are set out at the end of the book (*see* pages 132 and 145).

CHAPTER SEVEN

CONCLUSION

This is a book that not only suggests a wide range of activities for the pre-school child but also shows *why* these activities should be included and why they should be introduced in a certain order. It suggests that as your child develops and exercises the ability to transform knowledge into clear mental pictures, he or she will improve concentration, memorise better and improve the depth and speed of their thinking. There are difficulties because every child is an individual and comes from their own individual environment. It is also true that no parent would allow his or her influence to deny their child basic liberties. If control is too great, no pre-school child will develop their own personality. The notion of a world peopled by a robotic intelligentsia is repugnant and certainly the advancement of the human race would be hindered considerably.

The activities suggested in this book are not a blueprint for the whole mind. They represent knowledge upon which academic work can be based and will thrive. They certainly will not take up much of your or your child's time. Many represent what mother or father would encourage anyway in the course of being a good parent. However, the aim of this book is also to make a parent *conscious* of what they are doing when they say things to their child and to point out 'sins of omission', and to prove that what is not done before six will be reflected in that person in later years. Above all, we as parents are guardians of our children's thoughts and thinking and custodians of their talent. What we do not discover may never be discovered and ultimately we may be responsible, perhaps, for overlooking another Einstein or Beethoven, because we are too tired or too busy with our own interests, to devote a little extra time and attention to our children.

TESTS

The perfect mental 'image' is three-dimensional and embraces in some way all the senses. We can see the shape of an orange, smell it, feel it, dissect it, and taste it. Any assessment of a child's schemata or group of related concepts at pre-school stage should include this multiplicity of the senses. The tests below include only long-term memory because this is the most important in school life.

Long-Term Aural Memory

Set up a selection of common, distinct sounds in a particular order. For children aged three to four years wait two days and for children of five to six years wait four days and then see if your child can remember the order. He should close his eyes as you produce the sounds. An arrangement of five sounds is sufficient. Ask him to 'visualise' the sounds. Select from the following list: whistle, bell, dog bark, tap (with a ruler), scrubbing (with a brush), splashing water, the sound of a musical instrument. If your child gets three in order this is *good*; four in order is *excellent* and five in order is *exceptional*.

Long-Term Visual Memory

Take five items and place them in various parts of the room. Using the same time interval as for the Aural Memory Test above, see if your child can remember what article is paired with which piece of furniture. Select from the following lists:

Articles: marble, spectacles, pen, cup, book, spoon, comb
Furniture: on the television, on the shelf, on the table, on a chair, on the fridge, on his bed, in the bath

Your child should close his eyes and visualise the pairings one by one. Give two points for each success. Ten points is excellent. No points represents a poor long-term visual memory.

Senses of Smell, Taste and Touch

Your child should be able to define each sensation in some way (i.e. he must be able to *tell* you that a smell is, say, disinfectant). Set up an order of sensations: three for three- to four-year-olds and four, for five- to six-year-olds. Two days is long enough for a time interval. Make sure he closes his eyes and visualises. Here are some ideas:

Smell: orange, sausages or bacon cooking, strong-smelling sweets (e.g. mints), perfumed soap, disinfectant
Taste: orange, meat, sweets, chocolate, cake, nuts, sugar
Touch: plasticine, cloth, table-top, water, ball

Full score indicates excellent memory for that sensation.

Music

Two simple tests will give a good idea of ability:

a) *Singing in tune*: Can he sing a song he knows in tune, or reproduce one that you play or sing?

b) *Can he beat to time?* Show him how to do this and see if he
can continue.

Art

Some children who eventually become excellent artists produce
precocious drawings of a man. However, this is not always the
case: some simply seem to mature quicker than others physically, or have learnt from pictures they have seen. The same can
be said for children who begin to draw letters at an early age.
Often, those who develop quickly physically show good ability
to reproduce letters from three years on while others struggle.

Word Meanings and Numbers

Test your child on his ability to sort objects for size, shape and
colour. You will then have a good idea of what he knows. For
example, he may only know two colours well and needs to learn
the remaining ones.

Using pictures

On the following pages five pictures are reproduced. Each one
can be used to test both knowledge of word meanings and
number sense and suggested words are listed under each picture. Test your child on concrete words, actions and a few
abstract words. Ask, 'What is this?' and 'What is he doing?'

(*Parent Note* You will often need to rephrase questions so that
your child understands. All questions are dependent on age but
the aim is to establish what knowledge your child has. Only
then can it be built upon.)

New environments
These introduce new word meanings. For example a visit to the
sea-side will introduce a new range of knowledge and words
such as: sea, paddle, swim, float, boat, ship and so on. You can
test your child whenever you go into a new environment.

Picture 1

Telephone, doctor, boy, girl, tea-pot, cups, mixing, rolling, he, she, washing, bathing, wheel, driving, car, picture, doll, reading, writing, holding, push, carry, pencil, spoon, hat, hair, eye, mouth, nose, ear, shoe, trousers, dress, baby, mat, book, sit, stand, look, walk, help, talk, hand, foot, water, jumper

Picture 2

Skip, jump, cycle, pull, push, cry, climb, dig, run, sit, man, lady, rope, tree, wind, basket, hand, spade, sand, coat, socks, wheelbarrow, ball, gloves, outside, wall

Picture 3

Painting, cutting, wash, brush, blowing, bubbles, play, sand, building, bricks, racing, kneeling, box, cars, tap, pour, scissors, tip, table, chair, legs (of furniture), pictures, floor, teacher, kneel, point

Picture 4

Shop, pavement, pram, outside, road, across, lean,
carry, hold, hand, post-box, wave, scarf, fingers, gloves,
basket, bag, look, listen, stand, flowers, doorway,
window, open, in, entrance, exit, hat, cap, shoes, teddy,
arm, let, foot, chin, bags, Indian, Chinese, teeth, cheek,
old, young

Picture 5

Dinner, eat, drink, pour, shave, potato, fork, spoon,
knife, jug, cup, table, chair, wash, wipe, dry, hang, tie,
eat, shoe-lace, mirror, buttons, plants, rabbit, house,
smile, laugh, talk, toy, friend

TESTS FOR THREES TO FOURS

Test 1
Ask your child to name these concrete objects (change the order around):

bus, car, house, tree, hand, face (head), foot, shoe, hat, table, chair, knife, fork, spoon, plate, ball, dog, cat, bed, cup

cat

table

ball

tree

foot

hat

face

Test 2

Ask your child these questions:

'What is cold?' 'What is hot?' 'What is soft?' 'What is hard?'
'What is big?' 'What is small?' Any reasonable answer is
acceptable.

Test 3

This is a practical test. Ask your child to do the following:

(a) to build a bridge using several children's bricks

(b) to count from one to five using concrete objects

(c) to post shapes into a posting-box

(d) to build a tower using plastic cups and then to fit these into each other

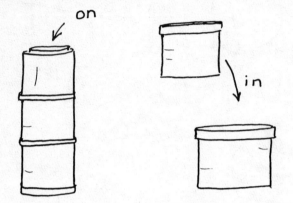

(e) to identify a colour when you ask him, 'What colour is this?' Concentrate in particular on yellow, red, blue and green.

(f) to complete a five-piece and then a nine-piece jigsaw

(g) to draw a cross and a man

TESTS FOR FOURS TO FIVES

Test 1
Ask your child to name these concrete objects (change the order around):

door, handle, lamp, television, clock, lamp-post, eye, nose, mouth, chin, hair, man, woman, book, shop, horse, pig

television

handle

door

lamp

woman

pig

shop

TOY SHOP

lamp-post

clock

man

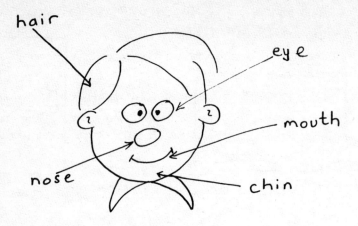

Test 2

Ask your child these questions:

'What is smooth?' 'What is rough?' 'What is high?'
'What is low?' 'What is day?' 'What is night?' 'What is fast?'
'What is slow?' 'What is long?' 'What is short?'
'What is round?'

Test 3

This is a practical test. Ask your child to do the following:

(a) to tell you the o'clock times on a clock face

(b) to count from one to 20 using concrete objects

(c) to identify more colours – include black, white, grey, orange, pink and purple

(d) to tie his laces, and to dress and undress on his own

(e) to draw Mummy, Daddy and a house

Test 4

Problems

(a) ask your child to set the table with plates, knives and forks (up to four or five place settings)

(b) ask him to share sweets equally between two or three dolls or teddies

(c) ask him to match socks and shoes correctly from piles of socks and shoes

(d) ask him to take a toy car on the shortest and longest routes on a plastic 'roadway'

(e) play 'Snap' with him to test speed of matching

(f) play notes on the piano and ask your child, 'Is this higher [or lower] than the last note?' Do not try notes too close together at first.

TESTS FOR FIVE PLUS

Test 1

Ask your child to name these concrete objects and actions (change the order around):

bird, elephant, run, jump, cry, punch, catch, under, over, up, down, hot, cold

jump

punch

cold

down

run

under

catch

over

bird

up

Test 2

Ask your child these questions:

'What is square?' 'What is straight?' 'What is bent?'
'What is a mother?' 'What is a father?' 'What is an uncle?'
'What is a grandfather?' 'What is a family?' 'What is a fruit?'
'What is a vegetable?' 'What is a bird?' 'What is an insect?'
'What jumps?' 'What hops?' 'What wriggles?'

Test 3

This is a practical test. Ask your child to do the following:

(a) to tell you the half-past times on a clock face

(b) to count money using 1p coins (with 2p or 5p coins is a bonus)

(c) to draw a man, a house and garden, grandma, a bus or a car

(d) to recite the alphabet

(e) to count up to 40 or 50 using buttons or beads on an abacus

Test 4

Abstract Work. Ask your child to do the following:

(a) to read these words: bus-stop, exit, danger, police

(b) to read these words: a, and, the, he, I, in, is, to, of, was, that (these are all key words). Then ask him to read: man, hat, dog, cat, run, cup, gun, bed, tap

(c) to copy or write down the letters of the alphabet and the numbers up to ten

Test 5

Problems

(a) ask your child to explain how to get to the shop/school (using different words – e.g. left, right, turn, straight, long way etc.)

(b) using 'Snap' cards, place in groups of twos. Sit with your child. Each of you turns up a pair. If they match, then shout

'Snap!' Turn down the pairs and continue until one of you remembers where a shown card matches one that has already been turned up. The winner keeps their pairs.

Test 6

Sums

Adding	$1 + 2 =$
	$2 + 3 =$
	$4 + 1 =$
	$2 + 0 =$
Taking away	$2 - 1 =$
	$3 - 2 =$
	$4 - 3 =$
	$5 - 0 =$

THE NATIONAL CURRICULUM

Tests for English And Maths

Age 7   Approximately level 2.
(*Note*   Some *number* targets are far exceeded by many pre-prep schools.)

Important attainment targets for English

Level 1   Recognise own name.
Recognise 'bus-stop', 'Exit', 'Danger'.
Begin to recognise individual words or letters.
Use of pictures, symbols, isolated letters
Difference between letters and numbers.
Write letter shapes in response to sounds.
Use single letters or letter groups to represent whole words.
Copying letters.

Level 2   Read labels on drawers and simple menus.
Knowledge of the alphabet.
Phonics.

Read a range of material.
Talk about a story.
Independent pieces of writing using complete sentences.
Capital letters, full stops, question marks.
Write stories with an opening and more than one character.
Other, simple writing.
Spell a range of common words including those *they* use
    commonly.
Recognise spelling patterns.
Produce capital and lower case letters.

Important attainments for Mathematics

Level 1   Numbers up to 10; counting, reading, writing and
    ordering. Addition, subtraction up to 10 (real objects).
Estimating number of objects up to 10.
Sorting 2-D and 3-D shapes.
Drawing 2-D shapes. Mapping diagrams. Repeating patterns.

Level 2   Numbers up to 100. Tens and Units.
Adding, subtracting up to 10.
'Difference'. Money in adding and subtracting.
Estimating number of objects up to 20.
Patterns in addition and subtraction up to 10.
Odd/Even. Symbol for a number.
Recognising shapes: square, rectangle, circle, triangle,
    hexagon, pentagon, cube, cuboid, cylinder, sphere.
    Notion of angle.
    Notion of translation, rotation, reflection.
    Frequency tables, block graphs.

TOYS, BOOKS, FILMS AND TAPES, AND OTHER USEFUL INFORMATION

TOYS AND PUZZLES

These lists are in addition to those suggestions in earlier chapters and are divided into the relevant subjects starting with those related to English and Mathematics or Number Skills. Toys are available from many *shops* but the largest concerns are: Beatties, Children's World, Early Learning Centre, John Lewis Partnership, Mothercare, W.H. Smith, Toys Я Us and Woolworths.

The main *toy manufacturers* to look out for are: Brio, Duplo and Lego, Fisher-Price, Galt Toys, Kiddicraft, Matchbox, Playmobil, Playskool, Spear's Games and Tomy.

A good set of *wooden learning bricks* is available from:
Home Education Centre
c/o CBS
Moor Lane
Bolton
Greater Manchester,
BL1 1AA

English
ABC Dot-to-Dot Books
ABC Sticker Books
ABC Wallchart (Ladybird Books, 1987)
Blackboard and chalks
Junior Scrabble (Spear's Games) Age 5–10
Ladybird Learning Frieze
Lights Alive Picture Maker (Tomy)
Lower Case Playdesk (Fisher-Price)
Spot's First Picture Word Cards (Michael Stanfield)
Word Perfect (Early Learning Centre). Use this to match words with
    pictures/word meanings

Mathematics and Number Skills
Abacus or Bead Frame (ten rows and ten beads)
Blackboard with chalks
Calculators (Casio, Sharp, Texas)
Chess – useful for helping memory
Clock with numbers clearly marked and movable hands
Computer and related games

Dot-to-dot books – to consolidate number recognition
Draughts – for spatial awareness, sense of angle and discipline
Geometric compass
'Little Professor' (Texas Instruments) – for practice in symbols such as
   +, −, ×, and tables
Magnetic or cling numbers
Musical Times Table tape
Number Dominoes

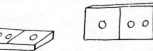

123 Sticker Books
Play money
Ruler with centimetres clearly marked
'Spot's First Pairs Game' (Michael Stanfield)
Tape measure
Times Table Frieze
Toy Cash Register
Weighing scales

Art and Creative Activities

Brushes – thick, long hog hair
Cartridge paper – all purpose
Chubbies – short, thick wax crayons (Early Learning Centre)
Collage kits – these contain a host of creative materials such as beads,
   straws, seeds, sticks, leaves, sticky paper, wool, cotton and glue
Coloured pencils – some are water-soluble and when dipped in water
   give a watercolour effect
Flower Press (e.g. Early Learning Centre)

Gummed shapes and Self-adhesive shapes – the Early Learning Centre has sets of dinosaur shapes, farm shapes and transport shapes. These really inspire creativity.

Modelling material such as plasticine and clay; also playdough either homemade (see page 78) or bought e.g. PlayDoh, Playstuff and the Early Learning Centre's Soft Stuff

Paint – the main colours needed are black, white (for mixing), yellow, red, blue and purple. Powder paints are available in tins (e.g. Berol, Early Learning Centre). Ready-mix paints are available in plastic containers (e.g. W.H. Smith, Galt, Early Learning Centre). Paint blocks. Finger paints are good for the younger child (e.g. Early Learning Centre).

Pastes (e.g. Polycell and Copydex for mounting). Glue sticks are also useful and are clean and quick (e.g. PrittStick).

Pencils – B is best, although HB is useful for Maths work and writing.

Press and Peel sets – a background scene with removable figures that cling (e.g. UniSet)

Printing sets

Rubbers/erasers

Scissors – a children's pair with blunt ends

Stencils and templates

Tracing paper

Constructional Toys

Basic Lego – look for the age range on the box

Construx – building system from Fisher-Price

Duplo

Meccano – for older children in the age group. Choose Meccano Set A made of plastic

Power workshop and tool kits

Sticklebricks – a first building brick from Playskool (especially Sticklebuddies)

Games

Some of these games will be suitable only for the more advanced children but it is worth trying them all.

Cluedo

Darts – use safety darts with blunted tips. Useful for scoring.

Happy Families

Hopscotch – useful for numbers

Marbles

Monopoly

Snap

Whist

Investigations

Binoculars (e.g. Fisher-Price, Galt Toys)

Globe

Magnets and sets such as Galt Toys' Magnet Building Set

Microscope and slides

Periscope

Music

Cassette recorder (Fisher-Price/Kiddicraft, Early Learning Centre)
Drum
Keyboard/Battery organ
Pocket radio or Two Tune TV (e.g. Fisher-Price)
Recorder
Xylophone (Glockenspiel)

Puzzles

Alphabet floor puzzle
Alphabet playtray
Jigsaws – wooden with five or more pieces and large-piece floor
   puzzles

Real-life Play (role models)

Doctor's set
Doll's house with play furniture, kitchenware etc. (e.g. Sylvanian from
   Tomy)

Kitchen centre (e.g. Fisher-Price)
Fireman's set
Nurse's set
Play house or play tent
Play people (Playmobil, Duplo and Lego)
Play sets such as a garage or an airport
Play telephone
Policeman's set
Post office set (e.g. Spear's Games or Petite)
Railway sets in wood (e.g. Brio)
Roadways – in carpet material for a playmat or separate cardboard
  pieces

BOOKS

This selective list is divided into the relevant stages for pre-school
children who will be learning to read through to information books
for the older child.

Picture Books

These are the best books for pre-school children to start with as they
have good illustrations to talk about and to stimulate interest.

Adams, Ken (illus. Val Biro), *When I was your Age*, Simon & Schuster
  1991
Ahlberg, Allan, *Happy Families* series, Viking Kestrel/Puffin; *Red
  Nose Readers*, Walker Books
Ahlberg, Janet and Allan, *Each Peach Pear Plum*, Oliver & Boyd
  1989; *Funny-Bones*, Heinemann 1980
Briggs, Raymond, *The Snowman* storybooks, Hamish Hamilton

Browne, Anthony, *Gorilla*, Julia MacRae Books 1983
Bruna, Dick, *I am a Clown*, Methuen 1976 (and other Bruna Books)
Burningham, John, *Avocado Baby*, Cape 1982; *Little Books* series,
  Cape
Carle, Eric, *The Very Hungry Caterpillar*, Hamish Hamilton 1970
De Brunhoff, Jean and Laurent, *Babar* books, Methuen/Magnet
Hill, Eric, *Spot* series, Heinemann
Hutchins, Pat, *Don't Forget the Bacon*, The Bodley Head 1976
Keats, Ezra Jack, *Whistle for Willie*, The Bodley Head 1966
Lodge, Bernard, *The Grand Old Duke of York*, Magnet
McKee, David, *Not Now, Bernard*, Andersen Press 1980. (A wonder-
  fully funny book, extremely appealing to young children – the very
  best picture book ever.)
Ross, Tony, *Naughty Nigel*, Andersen Press 1982
Sendak, Maurice, *Where the Wild Things Are*, The Bodley Head 1967
Vipont, Elfrida (illus. Raymond Briggs), *The Elephant and the Bad
  Baby*, Hamish Hamilton 1969
Zion, Gene, and Graham, Margaret Bloy, *Harry the Dirty Dog*, The
  Bodley Head 1960

More picture books are listed under the Early Readers section.

Rhymes and Fairy Stories

Boswell, Hilda, *A Treasury of Fairy Tales*, Collins; *A Treasury of
Nursery Rhymes*, Collins
Cole, Joanna, and Calmenson, Stephanie, compiled by, *The Read-
Aloud Treasury*, Michael O'Mara Books

Nursery Rhymes

Humpty Dumpty sat on a wall
Humpty Dumpty had a great fall
All the king's horses
And all the king's men
Couldn't put poor Humpty
Together again

The wheels on the bus

1. The wheels on the bus
   Go round and round
   Round and round, round and round
   The wheels on the bus
   Go round and round
   All day long

2. The wipers on the bus
   Go swish, swish, swish

3. Mummies on the bus
   Go chatter, chatter, chatter

4. Babies on the bus
   Go waah! waah! waah!

5. Grandmas on the bus
   Go "Oh, my back!
      Oh, my back!"

6. But the wheels on the bus
   Go round and round

Other rhymes

1. One, two buckle my shoe.
Three, four knock at the door.
Five, six pick up sticks.
Seven, eight open the gate.
Nine, ten a big fat hen.

2. Twinkle, twinkle little star
How I wonder what you are.
Up above the sky so high
Like a diamond in the sky.

3. Clap your hands together
One, two, three.
Put your hands upon your knee
Hurrah, hurrah!

4. Wind the bobbin up
Wind the bobbin up
Pull, pull
Wind it back again
Wind it back again
Point to the ceiling
Point to the floor
Point to the window
Point to the door.

Corrin, Sara and Stephen, Ed., *The Faber Book of Favourite Fairy Tales*, Faber 1988
Ladybird Book of Rhymes, Ladybird Books
Lines, Kathleen, Ed., (illus. Harold Jones), *Lavender's Blue: A Book of Nursery Rhymes* Oxford University Press
Nursery Rhyme Board Books, (illus. Moira Kemp), 1991; and *Action Rhymes Mini Books*, 1992, Simon & Schuster Young Books
Wildesmith, Brian, (illus. Moira Kemp), *Mother Goose Collection of Nursery Rhymes*, Oxford University Press 1964

Poetry

This is mainly for you to read to your child. There should be many pictures to stimulate his interest. Two very famous poems that always appeal to this and older age groups are 'Matilda Who Told Lies, and was Burned To Death' by Hilaire Belloc and 'Adventures of Isabel' by Ogden Nash, both from *A Catalogue Of Comic Verse*, edited by Rolf Harris (Hodder 1988). Other books to read to your child include:

Harrison, Michael and Clark, Christopher Stuart, Ed., *The Oxford Book of Christmas Poems*, Oxford University Press 1983; *The Oxford Treasury Of Children's Poems*, Oxford University Press 1988
Ireson, Barbara, Ed., *The Faber Book of Nursery Verse* 1983
McGough, Roger, and Rosen, Michael, *You Tell Me*, Viking 1989
McGough, Roger, Ed., *The Kingfisher Book Of Comic Verse*, Kingfisher 1986
Milligan, Spike, *Startling Verse for All The Family*, Penguin 1989
Nash, Ogden, *Custard and Company*, Blake, Quentin, Ed., Penguin 1981
Nicoll, Helen, Ed., *Poems For 7 Year Olds and Under*, Viking Kestrel 1985
Rosen, Michael, *Mind Your Own Business*, André Deutsch 1974

Learning to Read

Baby's First Board Book, (Blue Book and Pink Book) World International Publishing 1990. These are excellent for teaching letters and words.
Collins' *Beginner Books for Beginning Readers* series; *I Can Read it all by Myself*, Beginner Books series
Ladybird Books *Key Words* Reading Scheme (especially useful are the fairy story books)

World's Work *I Can Read* series (including Minarik, Else Holmelund, *Little Bear*, World's Work 1965)

Early Learners

(1) These books are for those children who have started to read well and need to consolidate. Picture books are the best books for this age group since they have good illustrations to provoke discussion and they often have fairly difficult words in the text. Authors to watch out for include:

Ahlberg, Janet and Allan (various publishers)
Murphy, Jill (Walker Books and others). (Her *Elephant Family* series is beautifully painted.)
Potter, Beatrix, *Peter Rabbit* books and others (Frederick Warne). These are classics and small children love them. The presentation of the books is the key to their success.

(2) Other authors and books with more substantial text that your child should try include:

Blyton, Enid. She wrote the equivalent of 800 children's books but is looked down on by many so-called reading 'experts'. However, children love her books and they are good easy-read books to stimulate interest in reading in general.
Dahl, Roald, *Fantastic Mr. Fox*, Allen and Unwin, 1970; *James and the Giant Peach*, Unwin Hyman 1990; *The Magic Finger*, Unwin Hyman 1989. Roald Dahl's books are extremely popular with children but can be a little sinister.
Edwards, Dorothy, *My Naughty Little Sister*, Methuen 1969; *More Naughty Little Sister Stories*, Methuen 1971
Hughes, Shirley (Walker Books and others)
Milne, A.A., *The World Of Pooh*, Methuen 1926
Murphy, Jill, *A Bad Spell for the Worst Witch*, Viking Kestrel 1984; *The Worst Witch Strikes Again*, Viking Kestrel 1988
Storr, C., *Clever Polly and the Stupid Wolf*, Penguin 1967 (perhaps the funniest short children's book)

Information Books

(1) Early Concepts
Ladybird Books and many other publishers provide ready access to books covering early concepts through all major book stores and your

Food

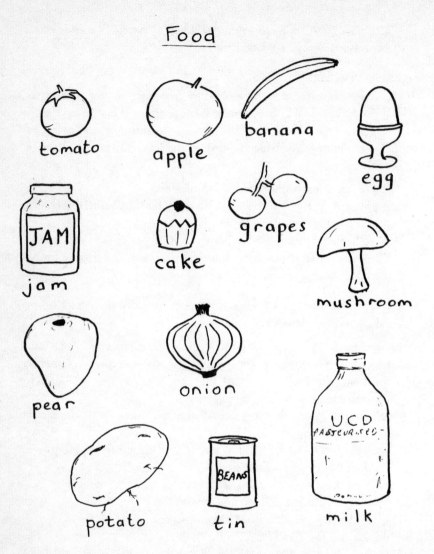

tomato

apple

banana

egg

JAM

jam

cake

grapes

mushroom

pear

onion

potato

tin

BEANS

UCD
PASTEURISED

milk

local public library. The subjects that should be covered are:
colours, early counting, phonics, shapes, opposites,
names of concrete objects (e.g. food, family),
names of activities (e.g. running, walking etc)

A comprehensive list of activities for the pre-school child is provided in:

Adams, Ken, *Your Child can be a Genius and Happy*, Thorsons 1988

General Concepts:
Speed — fast and slow

run
fast
quick
sprint

walk
slow

Position — inside and outside

inside
in
between
middle
squash

outside
out
around

(2) General Books

There is a wealth of excellent, beautifully produced information books from many publishers so it would be unfair and very difficult to select a book from each non-fiction category. However, certain books do stand out from the crowd. For the pre-school child you will, of course, need to read these to him at first.

Attenborough, David, *Discovering Life on Earth*, Collins 1981
McFarlene, D., Ed., *Guinness Book of Records*, Guinness 1990
Usborne *Spotter's Guides* (e.g. *The Seashore, The Weather, Dinosaurs, Fishes*)
Usborne *Mysteries and Marvels* series

It seems a tall order but you will need books in the house on every subject to stimulate and 'feed' your child's growing mind. A good encyclopedia with a large number of illustrations (such as *The Dorling Kindersley Children's Illustrated Encyclopedia* 1991) will help but individual subject books usually have better pictures. Your local public library is a good source of such books. The following is a list of subjects to look out for:

(a) Topics covered by Level 2 (up to age 7) of the National Curriculum for Science

The variety of life: garden animals and birds, insects, fish, flowers, fruit and vegetables, trees, zoo animals, the sea-side

Parts of the body

Other topics: health and hygiene, rubbish and waste products, squashing, stretching, bending, stopping, heating and cooling, the seasons and weather, magnets, sounds, colours, biggest to smallest

You can find more details about relevant topics in:

Adams, Ken, *Your Child can be Top of the Class*, Michael O'Mara Books 1991

(b) Other subjects that may interest your child

Foreign countries, space, famous people, bible stories, maps, rivers, mountains, dinosaurs, sharks, animals, birds, reptiles, mammals

(3) History

There are many excellent series available most ostensibly for older children but useful reference when your child has a query from school, or as a follow-up to a television programme. One such series is:

The Illustrated History Of The World, 8 volumes (fully illustrated), Simon and Schuster Young Books 1991 and 1992: Earliest Civilisations, Rome And The Ancient World, The Dark Ages, The Middle Ages, The Age Of Discovery, Conflict And Charge, The Nineteenth Century, The Modern World

Competent School Starters

Bond, J.M., *Assessment Papers* (English and Maths) 1st-4th Year Papers, Macmillan 1983. (Difficult but very advanced infants can begin these after the age of six.)

Hesse, K.A., *Graded Arithmetic Practice*, Books 1–4, Longman 1970/ 71

Newton, David, and Smith, David, *Practice in Basic Skills: English*, Books 1–5, Collins 1978/79; *Maths* Books 1–5, Collins 1978/80. The Book 1 *Basic Skills* books are fairly easy and your child should be competent at Book 2 before tackling the excellent series of *Assessment Papers in Reasoning*.

Schonell, Frederick J., *Essential Read-Spell* series, Macmillan 1977/ 83; *Essential Spelling List*, Macmillan 1932; *Essentials in Teaching and Testing*, Macmillan 1985

All schoolwork for ages five to 11, with tests, is covered in my previous book *Your Child can be Top of the Class*, Michael O'Mara Books 1991.

FILMS AND TAPES

Many films are now available on video tape affording easy access to some excellent films. Some suggestions are listed below.

Walt Disney films:

Alice in Wonderland, Bambi, Bedknobs and Broomsticks, Chitty-Chitty-Bang-Bang, Cinderella, Dumbo, Fantasia, Jungle Book, Lady and the Tramp, The Little Mermaid, Mary Poppins, 101 Dalmatians, Sleeping Beauty, Snow White, Songs of the South

In addition to these there are many real-life adventures to look out for.

Other films

Gulliver's Travels (the musical version), *The Wizard of Oz* (Judy Garland films)

The above films provide a rich store in memory to draw on for early story writing. The stories are more memorable because of the music throughout the films – enchanting songs such as 'Chim-chiminee', 'Feed the Birds', 'A spoonful of sugar', 'Supercalifragilistic', 'Zippidee-doo-dah', 'Hi-ho', 'Some day my prince will come', 'Faithful forever', 'All's well', 'When you wish upon a star', 'I got no strings', 'Hi-diddly-dee', 'We are Siamese if you please', 'Bibbidee-bobbodee-boo', 'Bella notte', 'Somewhere over the rainbow', 'We're off to see the Wizard', 'Ding-dong the witch is dead', 'Drip drip drop little April showers', 'I'm the King of the jungle', and the dramatic classical music from *Fantasia* (e.g. 'Night on a Bare Mountain') to name just a few.

Educational films

Those videos listed below can be obtained from W.H. Smith and other High Street shops or libraries:

Classic Nursery Rhymes (Watershed Pictures)
Golden Treasury of Nursery Rhymes (Abbey Broadcast Communications)
Learn with Sooty Series, *Start to Read, Simple Science, A-Z of Animals*, etc. (Abbey Broadcast Communications)
Nursery Rhymes (Pickwick Pictures Video)
Playbox (pre-school learning) (Central Independent Television)
Postman Pat's ABC Story, 1–2–3 Story (Tempo Video/W.H. Smith)
Sesame Street, Early Learners: *Learning about numbers* (Random House Inc). The very best pre-school videos.
Spot videos: *Spot's Alphabet, Spot Learns to Count*, by Eric Hill (Abbey Broadcast Communications)

Tapes with Books

Disney Read Along Collection with songs (Pickwick)
Hughes, Shirley books on tape (Picture Lions/Collins audio)
Postman Pat Easy Reader Series (Collins audio)
Tell a Tale Classic Stories (Ladybird Books)

A Selection of Computer Software – Tapes

BBC
Astronomy (BBC Soft)
Basic Maths (Aztec Software)
The Best 4 Maths (ASK Software)
Decimals (Chalksoft)
Early Learning (BBC)
Fractions (ISMEC)
Happy Letters (Bourne Education)
Happy Numbers (Bourne Education)
Let's Count (Acornsoft/ASK)
Maths with a Story, 1 & 2 (BBC Soft)
Money Plus 1, 2, 3, 4, (8–12 years) (Fernleaf)
Norman England, 1, 2, 3, 4 (Fernleaf)
Number Games (BBC Soft)
Number Puzzles (Acornsoft/ASK)
Number Skills 0–20, 0–999 (Longman)
Sentence Sequencing (Acornsoft/ESM Education)
Time man one, two (Bourne Education)
Viking England 1–4 (Fernleaf)
Words and Pictures (Chalksoft)
Words, words, words (Acornsoft)

Commodore
First Numbers (Collins)
First Moves (Longman)
Let's Count (Commodore 64)

Number Builder (Commodore 64)
Number Puzzler (Commodore 64)
Tony Hart's Art Master (Commodore 64)
Words & Pictures (Chalksoft)
Word Wobbler (*Spelling*) (Longman)
Words, words, words (Commodore 64)

Electron
The Best 4 Maths (ASK Software)
Chess (Acornsoft)
First Moves (Longman)
Happy Numbers (Bourne Education)
Let's Count (Acornsoft)
Number Puzzler (Acornsoft/ASK)
Picture Puzzler (LCL)
Words, words, words (Acornsoft/ASK)

Spectrum
a . . . b . . . c . . . Lift-off! (Longman)
Count about (Longman)
First Moves (Longman)
First Numbers (Collins)
Nursery Rhyme Adventure (Collins)
Sum Scruncher (Longman)
Super Writer (Collins)
Words and Pictures (Chalksoft)

PLACES TO TAKE YOUR CHILD

What follows is a list of specific places about Britain. These are in addition to trips to towns, sports centres, markets, farms, the sea-side, the countryside and local places of interest. The National Trust and English Heritage have many interesting properties throughout the country. Do not overload your young children with too much detail: you will need to work from a general concept and point out the variety, say, of *swords* on display at a castle (e.g. Belvoir Castle in Leicestershire) and explain simply when they were used in history and by whom. What a child learns at this age represents only a portion of a group of related concepts and its links. It takes time to develop such bodies of knowledge.

Castles and Stately Homes

Northern England

Alnwick Castle, Northumberland. 11th-century but restored in the 19th. Many treasures including Meissen china and paintings.

Bamburgh Castle, Northumberland. Norman but restored in the 19th century. Fine Hall and armoury. Dramatic position.

Castle Howard, Malton, North Yorkshire. Built by Sir John Vanbrugh 1700–37. Famous collections of furniture, porcelain, paintings and exhibition of costume.

Dunstanburgh Castle, Embleton, Northumberland. Ruined castle partly built by John of Gaunt, stands 100 feet above the sea.

Fountains Abbey and Studley Royal, Ripon, North Yorkshire. Abbey founded in 1132 and was the focal point for the gardens at Studley with its 400-acre deer park.

Holker Hall and Gardens, Cumbria. 16th-century house but rebuilt in the Victorian style. Many attractions.

Lindisfarne Castle, Holy Island, Northumberland. 16th-century castle restored in 1903 by Lutyens.

Rievaulx Abbey, North Yorkshire. Building began in 1132. Beautiful site.

Tatton Park, Cheshire. 16th-century house and deer park. Notable Georgian Hall. Tenants' Hall houses hunting trophies, veteran vehicles etc.

Central England

Belvoir Castle, near Grantham, Leicestershire. Rebuilt after a fire in 1816. Many treasures and paintings by masters.

Chatsworth, near Baslow, Derbyshire. Magnificent mansion with notable grounds, seat of the Devonshire family.

Ludlow Castle, Shropshire. Norman, built of beautiful pink sandstone.

Nottingham Castle, Nottinghamshire. Now a museum and art gallery. Robin Hood Exhibition. Underground passages.

Rockingham Castle, Market Harborough, Northamptonshire. Norman. Magnificent Banqueting Hall from the reign of Edward I.

Warwick Castle, Warwickshire. Very fine medieval castle with 17th-18th century mansion and extensive grounds and park.

Woburn Abbey, Bedfordshire. Original house 1145 rebuilt in the 18th century. Gardens, Safari Park and many attractions.

London and the South-East

Greater London:

Hampton Court Palace. Cardinal Wolsey began building in 1514. Became a royal residence in 1529. Much history. Maze and real tennis court.

Osterley Park, Isleworth. Tudor house reconstructed by Adam.

Syon House, Isleworth. Rebuilt by Adam in the 18th century on the site of a 15th-century nunnery. Garden by Capability Brown.

Tower of London, EC3. Built by William the Conqueror. Guarded by Yeoman Warders. Crown jewels and many exhibits.

Kent, Surrey, East and West Sussex

Arundel Castle, West Sussex. Originally 11th-century but much restored. Wealth of treasures.

Bodiam Castle, East Sussex. Moated 14th-century castle built to protect England from French invaders.

Dover Castle, Kent. A great Norman Castle with Roman pharos.

Hever Castle, Edenbridge, Kent. Moated, medieval castle where Henry VIII met Anne Boleyn.

Leeds Castle, near Maidstone, Kent. Said to be the 'Most beautiful castle in the world'. 9th-14th-century. Dog Collar Museum.

Loseley House, near Godalming, Surrey. Elizabethan (1562) built by Sir William More.

Petworth House, West Sussex. Built 1688–96. Magnificent collection of paintings. Park landscaped by Capability Brown.

Rochester Castle, Kent. Norman keep and cathedral.

Southern England

Beaulieu, Hampshire. Ruins of Cistercian Abbey (1204). Lord Montagu's National Museum of Veteran and Vintage Cars.

Blenheim Palace, Woodstock, Oxfordshire. Given to the Duke of Marlborough in 18th century. Imposing Palace with 2,500-acre Park.

Carisbrooke Castle, Newport, Isle of Wight. Fine Norman castle. Donkey-powered bucket well. Medieval wall.

Hatfield House, Hertfordshire. Palace built in 15th century. Rebuilt by Robert Cecil 1607–11. Very splendid Jacobean house.

Longleat, Warminster, Wiltshire. Everything from science to history. Mansion built 1559–78 set in grounds landscaped by Capability Brown which now include a Safari Park, a maze, boating lake and much else.

Maiden Castle, near Dorchester, Dorset. Britain's greatest prehistoric fort covering over 100 acres.

Portchester Castle, Portsmouth, Hampshire. Roman and Norman castle. Best Roman remains in Europe. 12th-century church.

Wilton House, Wiltshire. Designed by Inigo Jones in early 17th century. Seat of the Earls of Pembroke.

Windsor Castle, Berkshire. Home of kings and queens for 900 years. Founded by William the Conqueror. St George's Chapel is 15th-century. Safari Park nearby.

South-West England

Buckland Abbey, Yelverton, Devon. 13th-century monastery bought by Sir Francis Drake.

Dunster Castle, Somerset. 11th-century, re-modelled.
Pendennis Castle, Falmouth, Cornwall. Built by Henry VIII.
St Mawes Castle, Truro, Cornwall. Built by Henry VIII opposite Pendennis.
Sherborne Castle, Dorset. Castle partly built by Sir Walter Raleigh, 1594.

East Anglia
Blickling Hall, Norfolk. Early 17th-century house, famous Long Gallery. Dramatic yew hedges in gardens.
Castle Acre Priory, near Swaffham, Norfolk. Extensive earthworks once occupied by Normans, Romans and Saxons. Also ruins of Norman castle.
Holkham Hall, Norfolk. Splendid Palladian mansion 1734–60 with park by Capability Brown.
Ickworth House, Horringer, Suffolk. The house has a central rotunda and fine collection of silver and paintings. Extensive parkland.
Wimpole Hall, near Cambridge, Cambridgeshire. Spectacular brick mansion built in 1640 but altered in 18th century. Splendid rooms. 360 acres of parkland designed by Capability Brown and Humphry Repton.

Scotland
Balmoral Castle, Grampian. Grounds and Exhibition. On Royal Deeside. Queen Victoria first rented the castle in 1848 and today it is still the Queen's Highland residence. Prince Albert bought the castle and estate in 1852.
Blair Castle, Tayside. 13th-century castle but altered in the 18th century. Fine collection of portraits and many other treasures. Extensive grounds and deer park. Numerous events.
Culzean Castle, Strathclyde. 18th-century mansion and country park.
Edinburgh Castle, Lothian. 11th-century. Military tattoo late August.
Floors Castle, Kelso, Borders. Designed by Vanbrugh in 1718. Seat of Duke of Roxburghe. Magnificent gardens.
Glamis Castle, Tayside. Splendid 17th-century castle and childhood home of the Queen Mother. Fine collections. Events in the summer.
Palace of Holyrood House, Edinburgh, Lothian. Dating from 1500. Many relics and portraits.
Scone Palace, Tayside. The Kings of Scotland were crowned here until 1651. Magnificent collections of porcelain, furniture, ivory, clocks. Gardens (rhododendrons) and pinetum.

Stirling Castle, Central. Dramatic position. Built between 13th and 17th centuries.

Urquhart Castle, Highland. 14th-century castle overlooking Loch Ness. Once Scotland's largest castle.

Wales

There are many castles to see. Here are just a few:

Cardiff Castle, Clwyd. Norman castle dating from 1310.

Caernarfon Castle, Gwynedd. Built by Edward I on the Menai Strait. Moated ruins. Scene of Prince of Wales' Investiture 1969.

Conwy Castle, Gwynedd. Built 1283–87 by Edward I. Eight drum towers.

Chirk Castle, Clwyd. Castle walls and towers have survived since 1310. Dungeons.

Harlech Castle, Gwynedd. Splendid castle built by Edward I.

Powis Castle, Welshpool, Powys. Seat of the Herberts since the 16th century. Castle dates from 13th and 16th centuries. Beautiful gardens modified by Capability Brown.

Northern Ireland

Carrick Fergus Castle, Co. Antrim. Imposing Norman castle now a military museum.

Castle Coole, Enniskillen, Co. Fermanagh. Very fine Classical mansion (1789–95). Beautiful Regency furniture.

Drumena Castle, Castlewellan, Co. Down. Well-preserved Norman ring fort.

Dundrum Castle, Newcastle, Co. Down. Very fine medieval castle.

Harryville Castle, Ballymena. Co. Antrim. Very fine example of a Norman fort.

Cathedrals and Abbeys

The following are of particular interest and all date from the 11th and 12th centuries: Bangor, Bath, Bristol, Canterbury, Carlisle, Chester, Chichester, Durham, Ely, Exeter, Gloucester, Hereford, Norwich, Oxford, Peterborough, Ripon, Rochester, St Albans, St Asaph, St David's, St Paul's London, Salisbury, Southwark, Southwell, Wakefield, Wells, Westminster in London, Winchester, Worcester, York.

Museums and Other Places Of Interest

Northern England

Barnard Castle, Co. Durham. Bowes Museum and gardens.

Beamish, Co. Durham. North of England Open Air Museum – 200-acre site of buildings, rolling stock, farm machinery, colliery etc.

Halifax, West Yorkshire. Eureka! Children's Museum.

Hawkshead, Cumbria. Beatrix Potter Gallery.

Housesteads, Northumberland. Hadrian's Wall and Roman fort including famous Roman Hospital and latrines.

Liverpool, Merseyside. Liverpool Museum and Walker Art Gallery.

Macclesfield, Cheshire. Jodrell Bank Science Centre and Tree Park, with the Lovell 250-foot radio telescope (one of the largest fully steerable in the world) and Planetarium shows.

Manchester, Greater Manchester. Manchester Museum and Whitworth Art Gallery, Museum of Transport. Urban Heritage Park with Roman fort, Air and Space Museum and Museum of Science and Industry.

Newcastle upon Tyne, Tyne and Wear. Bagpipe Museum. John George Joicey Museum of local history, the Hancock Museum of Natural History, Museum of Science and Engineering, *Turbinia* (ship, 1890s), and others.

Sheffield, South Yorkshire. City Museum and Mappin Art Gallery, Abbeydale Industrial Hamlet.

York, North Yorkshire. Jorvik Viking Centre (time warp), National Railway Museum, Yorkshire Castle Museum and gardens, Undercroft Museum at York Minster.

Central England

Bedford, Bedfordshire. Museum.

Bromsgrove, Hereford and Worcester, Avoncroft Museum of Buildings.

Derby, Derbyshire. Industrial Museum, Royal Crown Derby Porcelain Co. Museum, City Museum and Art Gallery.

Birmingham. West Midlands. Museum of Science and Industry, City Museum and Art Gallery. Cathedrals. Railway museum.

Leicester, Leicestershire. Leicestershire Museum and Art Gallery.

Nottingham, Nottinghamshire. Robin Hood Centre, Wollaton Park, several museums of social history and industry. Museum of Costume and Textiles, the Lace Centre, Newstead Abbey (Byron's house).

Stratford-upon-Avon, Warwickshire. World of Shakespeare Museum, Shakespeare Centre, Nash's House, Anne Hathaway's Cottage, Mary Arden's House, Theatre Museum, Motor Museum, Teddy Bear Museum.

Telford, Shropshire. Ironbridge Gorge Museum – open air museum devoted to the Industrial Revolution Sites preserved *in situ* with Darby's original furnace at Coalbrookdale.

London and the South-East

Greater London:

Bethnal Green Museum of Childhood, E2

British Museum, WC1

Geological Museum, SW7

Guinness World of Records, The Trocadero, W1

Imperial War Museum, SE1

London Dungeon, SE1

The London Planetarium, NW1

London Toy and Model Museum, W2

London Transport Museum, WC2

Madame Tussaud's, NW1 (waxworks)

Museum of London EC2

Museum of Mankind, W1

National Army Museum, SW3

National Maritime Museum, SE10

National Postal Museum, EC1

Natural History Museum, SW7

Pollock's Toy Museum, W1

Royal Air Force Museum, NW9

Science Museum, SW7

Space Adventure, SE1

Telecom Technology Showcase, EC4

Victoria and Albert Museum, SW7

Wallace Collection, W1

Brighton, East Sussex. The British Engineerium.

Canterbury, Kent. Canterbury Heritage, Roman Pavement, Canterbury Pilgrims Way (audio-visual) and others.

Chichester, Singleton, West Sussex. Weald & Downland Open Air Museum. Good examples of vernacular architecture re-erected.

Southern England

Gloucester, Gloucestershire. National Waterways Museum, City Museum, Folk Museum, Regimental Museum, Beatrix Potter Centre.

Gosport, Hampshire, HMS *Alliance*, Submarines Museum, Fort Brockhurst.

Oxford, Oxfordshire. Ashmolean Museum of Art and Archaeology.

Portsmouth, Hampshire. HMS *Victory, Mary Rose* Exhibition, Royal Navy Museum, Cathedral, City Museum, D-Day Memorial and Museum, Royal Marines Museum, Natural Science Museum and Aquarium, Fort Widley.

Reading, Berkshire. Museum of English Rural Life. Ure Museum of Greek Archaeology, Cole Museum of Zoology.

Stansted Mountfichet, Hertfordshire. The House on the Hill Toy Museum.

Tring, Hertfordshire. Zoological Museum (part of the British Museum).

Windsor, Berkshire. Household Cavalry Museum. Madame Tussaud's display of Queen Victoria's Diamond Jubilee.

South-West England

Bath, Avon. Roman Baths Museum, No. 1 Royal Crescent, Museum of Costume and Assembly Rooms, The American Museum, Bath Industrial Heritage Centre (Mr Bowler's Business), Bath Carriage Museum, Bath Postal Museum, Claverton Pumping Station, and other museums.

Bristol, Avon. City Museum, SS *Great Britain*, Maritime Heritage Centre, Industrial Museum, Harveys Wine Museum, The Exploratory Science Centre.

Dorchester, Dorset. County Museum, Dorset Regiment Military Museum, Dinosaur Museum (the only one in Britain), Tutankhamun Exhibition.

Plymouth, Devon. Armada Experience, City Museum, Plymouth Hoe.

Sherborne, Dorset. Castle Museum, Worldwide Butterflies, Lullingworth Silk Farm.

Truro, Cornwall. County Museum (mineral collection of note), Pottery and Old Kiln Museum.

Wimborne, Dorset. Priest's House Museum.

East Anglia
Cambridge, Cambridgeshire. University Museum of Archaeology and Anthropology.
Cockley Cley, Norfolk. Iceni Village and Museum.

Scotland
Culloden, Highland. Culloden Battlefield and Visitor Centre.
Edinburgh, Lothian. Museum of Childhood, National Museum of Antiquities, Scotland's Clan Tartan Centre, John Knox's House, Royal Museum of Scotland.
Glasgow, Strathclyde. Hagg's Castle (quiz sheets and exploration), The Burrell Collection, Hunterian Museum, Museum of Transport, Regimental Museum of Royal Highland Fusiliers, Victoria Park and Fossil Grove.
Loch Ness, Highland. Official Loch Ness Monster Exhibition Centre at Drumnadrochit, 40-minute computer-controlled presentation.
Melrose Abbey, Borders. Fine Cistercian abbey with museum.

Wales
Cardiff, South Glamorgan. National Museum of Wales, St Fagan's Folk Museum, Welsh Industrial and Maritime Museum.

Northern Ireland
Giant's Causeway, Co. Antrim. Dramatic rock formation on coast. A World Heritage site.
Omagh, Co. Tyrone. Melton House and Ulster-American Folk Park.

Art Galleries
London, National Gallery WC2, National Portrait Gallery WC2, Tate Gallery SW1.
Edinburgh, Lothian. National Gallery of Scotland.
Glasgow, Strathclyde. Hunterian Art Gallery (Charles Rennie Mackintosh).
Manchester, Greater Manchester. City Art Gallery.

Zoos and Animal Parks

Northern England
Chester Zoo, Cheshire
Flamingo Land, Kirby Miseperton, North Yorkshire
Harewood Bird Garden, Harewood, West Yorkshire

Knowsley Safari Park, Prescot, Merseyside
Morecambe Marineland, Lancashire
Southport Zoo, Southport, Merseyside
Wildfowl Trust, Martin Mere, Lancashire, and Washington, Tyne and
   Wear

Central England
Dudley Zoo, West Midlands
Linton Zoological Gardens, Cambridgeshire
Long Sutton Butterfly Park, Lincolnshire
Malvern Hills Animal and Bird Gardens, Hereford and Worcester.
Riber Castle Wildlife Park, Matlock, Derbyshire
Skegness Natureland Marine Zoo, Lincolnshire
Stratford-upon-Avon Butterfly Farm and Jungle Safari with Insect
   City, Warwickshire
Twycross Zoo, Tamworth, Leicestershire.
West Midland Safari Park, Bewdley, Hereford and Worcester
Whipsnade Wild Animal Park, Dunstable, Bedfordshire
Woburn Wild Animal Kingdom, Bedfordshire

London and the South-East
Brighton Aquarium and Dolphinarium, East Sussex
Birdworld and Underwater World, Farnham, Surrey
Drusilla's Zoo Park, Alfriston, East Sussex
Gatwick Zoo, Charlwood, Surrey
Howletts Zoo Park, Bekesbourne, Kent

London Zoo, NW1
Syon Park Butterfly House and Jungle Safari, Brentford
The Wildfowl and Wetlands Centre, Arundel, West Sussex

Southern England
Child Beale Wildlife Trust. Basildon, Berkshire
Cotswold Wildlife Park, Burford, Oxfordshire
Isle of Wight Zoo, Sandown
Marwell Zoological Park, near Winchester, Hampshire
Windsor Safari Park, Berkshire

South-West England
Aqualand, Torquay, Devon
Butterfly Farm and Jungle Safari, Lodmoor Country Park, near
  Weymouth, Dorset
Combe Martin Wildlife Park, Devon
Cricket St Thomas Wildlife Park, Somerset
Cotwold Farm Park, Guiting Power, Gloucestershire
Dartmoor Wildlife Park, Plympton, Devon
Longleat Safari Park, near Warminster, Wiltshire
Newquay Zoo, Cornwall
Paignton Zoological and Botanical Gardens, Devon
Sea Life Centre, Weymouth, Dorset
Tropical Bird Gardens, Rode, near Bath, Avon
The Wildfowl and Wetlands Centre, Slimbridge, Gloucestershire
Worldwide Butterflies, Sherborne, Dorset

East Anglia
Banham Zoo and Monkey Sanctuary, Banham, Norfolk
Colchester Zoo, Essex
Norfolk Wildlife Park, Great Witchingham, Norfolk
The Otter Trust, Bungay, Suffolk
Suffolk Wildlife Park, near Lowestoft, Suffolk
The Wildfowl and Wetlands Centre, Welney, Norfolk

Scotland
Argyll Wildlife Park, Inveraray, Strathclyde
Blair Drummond Safari Park, near Stirling, Central
Butterfly Farm and Jungle Safari, Lasswade, near Edinburgh, Lothian
Edinburgh Zoo, Lothian

Glasgow Zoo, Uddingston, Strathclyde
Highland Wildlife Park, Kincraig, Highland
Sea Life Centre, Barcaldine, Strathclyde
The Wildfowl and Wetlands Centre, Caerlaverock, Dumfries and
  Galloway

Wales
Anglesey Sea Zoo, Brynsiencyn, Anglesey
Welsh Mountain Zoo, Colwyn Bay, Clwyd
The Wildfowl and Wetlands Centre, Llanelli, Dyfed

INDEX